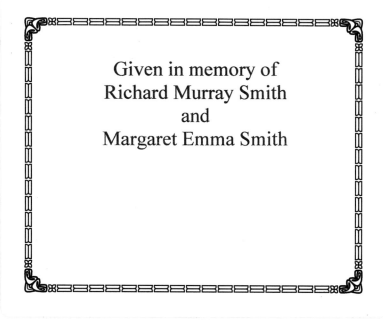

Given in memory of
Richard Murray Smith
and
Margaret Emma Smith

Lincoln's Table

A President's Culinary Journey
from Cabin to Cosmopolitan

Abraham Lincoln (artist unknown) and Mary Lincoln, painted by Katherine Helm.
(Townsend Collection of Mary Genevieve Townsend Murphy)

Lincoln's Table

A President's Culinary Journey
from Cabin to Cosmopolitan

Donna D. McCreary

With Foreword by
Kim Matthew Bauer

LINCOLN PRESENTATIONS

Published in the United States by

LINCOLN PRESENTATIONS
Charlestown, Indiana
www.marylincoln.com

ISBN-13: 978-0-9795383-1-5

ISBN-10: 0-9795383-1-9

Lovingly dedicated to my grandmother,
Elizabeth Ann Bruce Ellis,
who taught me the most important
ingredient is always love.
And to my mother,
Helen Lela Ellis McCreary,
who still makes the best pies
this side of Heaven.

Contents

❧

Foreword

Donna McCreary's second edition of her work, *Lincoln's Table*, is a wonderful update to the known collections of the recipes that graced the dining table of the Lincolns. While it focuses primarily on the dishes that Abraham Lincoln ate throughout his lifetime, it is also a commentary. Much like the Horatio Alger books of that period, *Lincoln's Table* allows the reader the luxury of tracing Lincoln's rise to prominence, a rise that is rife with the increasingly rich and varied meals that are present throughout Lincoln's life.

Yet this book is more than just a recipe book. It is also a type of social commentary. If the adage that the way to a man's heart is through his stomach is true, then it pays to give close attention to the many and diverse meals that Mary Lincoln brought to the table (pun intended) during her nearly twenty-three-year marriage to Abraham. This book helps to dispel the criticism that Mary Lincoln was parsimonious with her meal portions, that she was not a good cook, and that her sense of entertaining was driven by undue "finery." After all, if these criticisms had been true it then would beg the question of how she could bring together what Isaac Arnold would term a "grand feast" with the meal consisting not of the eastern establishment of "finery" but with the more common frontier fare of venison, wild turkey, and other game animals. No, what this book helps to show to students and scholars of Lincoln is that what drove Mary to her decisions was not how "well" she could cook, but rather for "whom" she wished to cook, a big difference in the world of the culinary arts.

In the end, what this book continues to do so well is to chronicle the life of Abraham Lincoln through the food he ate, from the simple fare of the frontier to the most elaborate meals that were befitting, well, a President. With more than sixty new recipes added to those from her first edition,

Donna McCreary has allowed the reader a glimpse into the dishes that literally made Abraham Lincoln the man he was. This insight allows for the reader to experience firsthand what was eaten by a man many consider the greatest American ever produced by this country. More significantly, it gives the reader a chance to become a part of that history, albeit gastronomically, through the preparation and eating of the foods presented in these recipes. So, enjoy the history, enjoy the insight, but most importantly enjoy the food. Bon appetit!

Kim Bauer
Director, Lincoln Heritage Project
City of Decatur, Illinois
March 10, 2008

Introduction

Why a Lincoln cookbook?

A common belief exists that Abraham Lincoln was a fussy eater and had little or no interest in food. Five months after his death, though, his stepmother, Sarah "Sally" Bush Johnston Lincoln, told William Herndon, Lincoln's law partner in Springfield: "Abe was a moderate eater and I now have no remembrance of his special dish: he sat down and ate what was set before him, making no complaint." [§]

She may not have remembered any special preferred dish, but her stepson did. As an adult he spoke of his mother's gingerbread and corn cakes; these foods remained among his favorites throughout his life. His cousin, John Hanks, who lived with the Lincoln family for a four-year period in Indiana, recalled some of Abe's eating habits: "[He] was a good and hearty eater—loved good eating. His own mother and stepmother were good cooks for them days and times." [§§]

Perhaps that is why Lincoln's stepmother never heard any complaints from him about anything she set on the table.

This book began as a search for some recipes that Lincoln enjoyed, to find a few things that could be prepared for school children and adults who were having "Lincoln-themed" parties and dinners. The recipe collection grew until it became large enough to publish the first edition of *Lincoln's Table* in 2000. Since then, however, the collection has continued to grow, resulting in this second edition: *Lincoln's Table: A President's Culinary Journey from Cabin to Cosmopolitan*. More than sixty recipes have been added—some historic,

---

[§] Holzer, *Lincoln As I Knew Him*, p. 16.

[§§] Ibid. p. 23.

some modernized versions—which represent foods that have been traced to Lincoln's dining table at some point in his life. That table may have been the rough-hewn one made by his father, or the beautiful, elaborate piece of furniture used for state dinners in the White House. Some of the dishes were savored by the Lincoln family in Springfield; others were relished in the homes of friends; in boarding houses; in fine New York restaurants; or in the elegant dining room of the White House. Regardless of their source, all of the foods represented here share one common distinction: they were enjoyed by Abraham Lincoln.

Lincoln's culinary journey was indeed a remarkable one. In the early nineteenth century when he was a child, food could be scarce in the Indiana and Kentucky wilderness, and the pioneers were often grateful for anything they had to eat, no matter how it was prepared. Any family boasting an accomplished or "good" cook tending to their meals was ensured satisfied appetites and happy palates. During Lincoln's youth, his family raised most of its food; meals were supplemented by fruit from trees that grew in the area and the wild berry bushes and vines that were abundant in the woods. The grains they harvested from their tilled fields were taken to a local mill to be ground into flour; corn was a staple. Honey, maple syrup, and sorghum were popular sweeteners for pioneers. Spices and other items could be purchased at a local store, such as the one owned by James Gentry of Gentryville, Indiana, or sometimes from traveling peddlers.

Bartering or trading was a common practice among pioneers. Lincoln once swapped fire wood for nine yards of white cloth—part of which was used to make the first white shirt he ever owned.[†] It was natural for neighbors to trade animals, produce, and even labor skills to provide a wider variety of foodstuff and supplies for their families.

Although many farmers such as Thomas Lincoln raised hogs, their primary source of meat was obtained by hunting and fishing. The Lincoln family dined on game such as venison, bear, squirrel, rabbit, opossum, and

---

† Donald, *Lincoln*, p. 34.

wild turkey. (Since these are not commonly found in today's grocery stores, recipes featuring wild game are not included in this book.)

Even as a young man, Abraham recognized the importance of the family cook. When his mother, Nancy Hanks Lincoln, died of milk sickness, the cooking responsibilities fell mostly upon his sister, Sarah. However, he surely assisted with some of the cooking chores and may have helped prepare meals. It is clear that in his early life, Lincoln did indeed learn some cooking skills, even if it was nothing more than roasting game meat on a stick over an open campfire.

Those skills proved valuable. Soon after the Lincoln family moved to Illinois, Denton Offutt hired Lincoln, John Hanks, and John T. Johnston to take a flatboat loaded with merchandise to New Orleans. This would be Lincoln's second trip to that city. The trio's first task was to build the flatboat at the river landing of Sangamo Town. Someone had to be responsible for preparing meals, and Lincoln was "elected cook, a distinction he never underestimated for a moment."§ Thus began his trek away from the food of his father's pioneer home and to a culinary journey on which he would become acquainted with a new world of flavors.

Some historians have written that Lincoln ate only to live and at times had to be reminded to do so. According to his secretary, John Hay, Lincoln ate merely an egg, toast, and coffee for breakfast. Lunch included a biscuit, glass of milk in the winter, some fruit or grapes in summer.§§

Noah Brooks, a family friend and a correspondent for the Sacramento *Daily Union*, noted: "[T]he president would appear to forget food and drink were needful for his existence, unless he were persistently followed up by some of the servants, or was finally reminded of his needs by the actual pangs of hunger. On one such occasion, I remember, he asked me to come in and take breakfast with him, as he had some questions to ask. He was evidently eating without noting what he ate; and when I remarked that he

---

§ Angle, *Life of Herndon's Lincoln*, p. 62.

§§ Wilson, *Herndon's Informants*, p. 331.

was different from most Western men in his preference for milk for breakfast, he said, eyeing his glass of milk with surprise, as if he had not before noticed what he was drinking, 'Well, I do prefer coffee in the morning, but they don't seem to have sent me any.' Who 'they' were I could only guess."§§§

Recalling a day during his six-month stay at the White House while painting *The First Reading of the Emancipation Proclamation*, Francis B. Carpenter best explained the president's eating habits. He told how, upon hearing the clock strike noon, Lincoln said: "I believe, by the by, that I have not yet had my breakfast, —this business has been so absorbing that it has crowded everything else out of my mind."§§§§

These observations examine only a fragment of Lincoln's life, and yes, indeed, the war did crowd Lincoln's mind. With his thoughts always on matters of state, day to day eating was often neglected. However, he did eat. Menus from White House dinners and parties give a glimpse as to what he ate and what he favored.

It is true that Lincoln was a lean man: His one hundred-and-eighty-pound weight was stretched over his six-foot four-inch body when he entered the White House. However, earlier in his life he had been described as fleshy and muscular, and some early photographs of him reveal a man who could easily be described as being barrel-chested. When he lived in New Salem, Lincoln's weight was at least two hundred and twenty pounds, and was probably near that during his early years as a Springfield lawyer. The gauntness that shows in his last photographs is an indication of the stress and strain of the Civil War, which sapped another twenty pounds from his frame by its end in 1865.

So again, one may ask, "Why a Lincoln cookbook?"

Because, despite popular belief, Lincoln did indeed enjoy good cooking

---

§§§ Brooks, *Washington, D.C., in Lincoln's Time*, pp.228–229.
§§§§ Carpenter, *The Inner Life of Abraham Lincoln*, p.34.

and had many favorite dishes. In addition to the gingerbread and corn cakes of his youth, he loved oysters, regardless of how they were prepared. He had a fondness for chicken, turkey, and beefsteak. Lincoln's sweet tooth craved pecan pie, lemon pie, a wide variety of cakes, and ice cream. As Lincoln's life journey took him from the cabin in the wilderness to the grace and elegance of the aristocracy, his menus became more refined. No longer were his meals constrained by what was available at the time. Menus now could be planned in advance. Many varieties of meat were available as well as foods to accompany them, and his choices indicated his favorites.

While traveling the Eighth Judicial District as a circuit lawyer, Lincoln stayed at several boarding houses. Legends abound about his enjoying a meal and asking the proprietor for recipes to take home to Mary. Lincoln often did some of the grocery shopping in Springfield, carefully selecting the meat for the evening meal. As President-elect, he ensured some of his favorites would be served by planning the menu for his first inaugural luncheon.

Elizabeth Todd Grimsley, Mary Lincoln's cousin, accompanied the Lincoln family to Washington[†] in 1861. She stayed the next six months to assist Mary with some of the official White House hostess duties and to accompany her on shopping trips to New York City. Years later, Mrs. Grimsley wrote about her visit and her intimate observances of her cousin's family, including recounts of state dinners, receptions, and leisurely breakfasts with family and friends from Illinois. She recalled one dinner when a physician was summoned afterward because everyone, including the President, was suffering from severe gastric pain. The cause turned out to be nothing more than an overindulgence in a tempting dish of Potomac shad.[††] Clearly, Lincoln had found another favorite dish.

In early March 1862, American author Nathaniel Hawthorne had a nine

---

[†] Up to and during the Lincoln administration the nation's capital was called "Washington" or "Washington City." For simplicity, "Washington" is used throughout the text of this book.

[††] Grimsley, "Six Months in the White House," *Journal of the Illinois State Historical Society*, vol. XIX, pp. 43–73.

A.M. appointment to meet President Lincoln. Not wanting to disrupt the President's schedule, Mr. Hawthorne was punctual. Lincoln was not. He sent word to his waiting guest that he was having his breakfast. Hawthorne wrote, "His appetite, we were glad to think, must have been a pretty fair one; for we waited about half an hour in one of the antechambers."[†††]

To answer the questions of why a Lincoln cookbook and why a second edition of such a book, one needs only to look at the culinary changes during Lincoln's life to understand the social changes he experienced. His climb from cabin to cosmopolitan enriched his dining experience. His eating utensils changed from carved drinking gourds and wooden bowls to European china and crystal stemware. His tasty morsels changed from wild game and cornbread prepared on an open fire to chef-inspired dishes sculptured to resemble baskets and military forts. The common denominator between all of these is that Lincoln enjoyed them. He relished them. And nourishing him, these foods gave him the energy to make that life journey from the pioneer cabin to the cosmopolitan of Washington. All are good food, meant to be enjoyed. So, grab a plate, pull up a chair, and enjoy a true taste of Lincoln history!

Donna D. McCreary
May 2008

[†††] Holzer, p. 166.

AUTHOR'S NOTE: Historic recipes often have few, if any, cooking instructions. Ingredients and preparation methods are sometimes unknown to modern cooks. Instructions may require equipment and supplies no longer available. Cooking was done on open hearths or cast-iron stoves fueled by wood. Ice cream was made in wooden buckets with turn cranks. Modern methods are included for convenience and time.

Recipes written for wood-stove baking often use terms such as "quick" or "moderate" oven. These terms are sometimes difficult to translate to modern appliances. Since ovens often vary, the cook should carefully monitor any historic recipe; check roasted and baked goods frequently and test for doneness. The cook may also wish to make notes for future reference as each recipe is prepared.

Modern bakers will find the following chart helpful.

Quick oven	400–450 degrees
Hot oven	375–400 degrees
Moderate oven	350–375 degrees
Slow oven	300–350 degrees
Cool oven	250–300 degrees

Kentucky

1869 – 1816

Representation of Lincoln's birth cabin in Hodgenville,
Kentucky. Illustration by Amy Castleberry.

When Thomas Lincoln married Nancy Hanks, Kentucky was the frontier. A family forged a living from the rich soil, growing crops, raising some domestic animals, and fishing and hunting wild game for food. It was a difficult life, but it was a good life for the Lincoln family and their Kentucky neighbors. Little is known about what the Lincoln family ate during the years they lived in Kentucky. Most all early cookbooks and family domestic books included recipes for preparing wild game such as deer, pheasant, turkey, quail, rabbit, squirrel, woodchuck, and even bear. The Lincoln family would have eaten some, if not all, of the various types of wild game available in the area. Presumably, Thomas Lincoln and his son went fishing. Nancy tended a garden, and the woods were full of wild berries, persimmons, cherries, pawpaws, and nuts.

In addition to feeding the adults, Nancy Lincoln had to feed her children, Sarah and Abraham.

Abraham Lincoln lived two places in Kentucky. The first was known as the Sinking Spring farm, located near Hodgenville. Thomas Lincoln had purchased the 348½ acres for cash in December of 1808, and with his wife, Nancy, and their daughter, Sarah, moved to the farm. On February 12, 1809, Abraham was born. For two years, Thomas Lincoln worked the land only to discover the man who sold him the property did not have clear title to it. The Lincoln family then moved to the Knob Creek farm a few miles away. Later, Lincoln wrote that his first memories were of the Knob Creek farm. It was here that he first remembered eating corn cakes for breakfast. According to Harriet A. Chapman, Lincoln's cousin, Lincoln often joked that he could "eat corn cakes twice as fast as two women could make them."[†] They continued to be his favorite breakfast and late Sunday supper dish throughout his life.

These are delicious with butter and maple syrup. These are best when eaten hot off the griddle, and a cold glass of buttermilk makes them even more Lincolnesque.

Knob Creek Corn Cakes

(Makes 32–36 two-inch cakes)

2	cups cornmeal
1	teaspoon salt
1	teaspoon soda
1	egg, lightly beaten
3	cups buttermilk

Sift together cornmeal, salt, and soda. Add the egg and buttermilk. Mix well to blend, but do not overbeat. (The batter should be thin enough to form a lacy edge when baking.) Drop by small spoonfuls on a hot griddle; cook till golden, turn, and finish cooking. Stack cakes on a cookie sheet and place in a 250 degree oven to keep warm.

[†] Wilson, *Herndon's Informants*, p. 512.

Cast-iron Cooking

Cooking with a cast-iron Dutch oven—a deep pot with a close-fitting lid—was popular in pioneer times, and still is today. Iron cookware is used by campers, re-enactors, and by outdoor enthusiasts. Proper care must be used to maintain these essential cooking utensils.

Before using a piece of iron cookery, it must be properly seasoned. This is done by rubbing lard, shortening, or beef suet over the entire surface of the inside of the pot. Place it in an oven at 150 degrees and leave for two hours. Prepare the outside of the pot in the same manner, and again, return to the oven for two hours. Remove from the oven, and allow the item to cool. Wash with warm, soapy water and dry well. Return the pot to the oven to dry (drying beside a campfire is often recommended).

After using an iron pot, wash it with warm, soapy water, and scrub well. Dry thoroughly either by hand, or by placing near a fire or in an oven. Never leave water standing in any cast-iron cooking vessel—rust will ensue. Also, never store iron cookware with its lid in place; doing so will allow the pot to trap moisture, thus causing a musty odor and rust spots.

The Lincoln family would have enjoyed a mug of buttermilk with these potatoes, thus making a hearty meal.

Nancy Hanks' Steamed Potatoes

(Serves 6–10)

6   to 10 medium-sized
      potatoes
1   cup water
      Salt and pepper
      Butter

Scrub potatoes well. Pile into an iron Dutch oven. Pour salted water over potatoes. Place the lid on the Dutch oven. On top of the lid, place several pieces of glowing charcoal or embers from a fire. (If cooking in a modern oven, preheat the oven to about 300 degrees.)

Steam potatoes slowly for about an hour or until they are tender. Do not lift the lid unless absolutely necessary. Serve potatoes in their jackets with salt, pepper, and butter.

This cake is served without icing. It is wonderful with a little powdered sugar sprinkled on the top, or served with whipped cream or ice cream.

Sorghum Cake

½   cup butter
1   cup sugar
1   slightly beaten egg
1   cup sorghum
3 ½ to 3 ¾ cups sifted flour
¼   teaspoon nutmeg
¼   teaspoon cinnamon
1   teaspoon baking soda
1   teaspoon baking powder
1   cup sour milk

Grease and flour a 13 by 9-inch cake pan. Preheat oven to 325 degrees.

Cream together butter and sugar. Slowly add the slightly beaten egg and sorghum. Beat mixture well. Sift all the dry ingredients together. Alternately add dry ingredients and the milk to the creamed mixture. When all ingredients are added, beat well. Pour batter into prepared pan and bake about 40–45 minutes, or until cake tests done. (This cake can also be baked in a bread pan, or a bundt cake pan. In such a case, increase the baking time to one hour.) Serves 8–10.

Proper Food for Children

Sarah Josepha Hale was a well-known writer during the nineteenth century. She was the editor of *Godey's Lady's Magazine* and was a leading factor in women's fashion, health, and social reform, known by almost every woman in American, and even by some men, including Abraham Lincoln. Hale is remembered today as the author of the poem "Mary Had a Little Lamb."

In her articles and books, Hale wrote to young mothers and new housekeepers. In the following excerpt from her book, *The Good Housekeeper* (published in 1841), Ms. Hale offered guidelines for ensuring good nutrition for children.

> *The milk of the mother ought in every instance to constitute the food of an infant, unless such an arrangement is impracticable. After the child is weaned, fresh cow's milk in which a small portion of soft water has been mingled, and sometimes a little sugar, with a small quantity of crust of bread softened, is usually the most healthy food; but this should be varied by occasional meals of gruel, arrow-root, or sago, and if the child is delicate and shows signs of acidity or flatulence, then a preparation of weak chicken broth or beef tea, freed from fat, and thickened with soft boiled rice, may be given.*
>
> *The same kind of food ought to be continued, with the addition of good bread (and potatoes, when well cooked, seem as healthy food nearly as bread), till the appearance of the "eye teeth"; when they are fairly through, a portion of soft-boiled egg, and occasionally a little meat, the lean part, well cooked and not highly seasoned, may be given.*

For older children with teeth, Hale wrote:

Ripe fruits should never be given to children till they have teeth, and unripe fruits ought never to be eaten.

During childhood and early youth, the breakfast and supper should consist principally of bread and milk, ripe fruits and vegetable food; it will be sufficient to allow a portion of animal food with the dinner.

Fish, chicken, and other white meats are best for children. Fat pork is nearly indigestible for the young and delicate, and ought never to be eaten by them.

Hale called for people to drink water as a safe beverage for all ages. A cup of warm tea was considered good for the stomach. It was advised for people to sip their water and not drink rapidly. Adults were encouraged not to drink cold water when they felt overheated or fatigued. It was believed to be bad for the digestive system and not a good source of quenching one's thirst. Water at room temperature, or warm tea was best in those conditions.

Children were instructed to drink more water and liquids than adults, but a habit of continual drinking was believed to weaken the stomach and render children irritable and peevish. During the cold months, children were encouraged to drink milk instead of their usual water. Mrs. Hale wrote, "Children should take milk—as a substitute, during the winter, good gruel with bread, or water, sweetened with molasses, is healthy. Never give children tea, coffee, or chocolate with their meals."

Indiana

1816 – 1830

Representation of Lincoln's Indiana home near Little Pigeon
Creek in Spencer County. Illustration by Amy Castleberry.

*E*ighteen-sixteen was known as "the year without a summer." § Mount Tambora, located in Indonesia, erupted in April 1815 and caused a severe cooling of the Northern Hemisphere that lasted well into the following year. Even in July of 1816, frost killed the crops and gardens of Kentucky families. In November of that year, Thomas Lincoln went to Indiana to purchase property. Land sold for less than three dollars per acre, and Thomas Lincoln purchased eighty acres in Hurricane Township of what was then Perry County. §§ He marked his property by placing huge piles of brush on each corner. He then constructed a half-faced cabin which his family would use as shelter for a few days while their cabin was built.

In December 1816 the Lincoln family began the five-day journey to their new home. This time they traveled ninety-one miles, and crossed the Ohio River by ferry to Bates Landing. From there, it was another sixteen miles to the homestead. Lincoln wrote, "We reached our new home about the time the State came into Union." According to Lincoln, Indiana was "a wild region, with many bears and other wild animals still in the woods." At night, they could hear the panthers scream. Here the family settled into a heavily wooded area that had to be cleared for crops, a home, a barn, and a garden. As Lincoln himself said, "Here I grew up."

Nancy Lincoln had thought about the cooking and eating needs of her family prior to the move to Indiana. For cooking chores and meal preparation she brought a cast-iron skillet or spider, a Dutch oven, a large kettle, and small pans. In addition to cooking equipment, some sort of eating utensils were also needed. A few wooden bowls, pewter dishes, knives and forks, and a few other simple utensils were

---

§ Conway, *Young Abe Lincoln: His Teenage Years in Indiana*, p. 7.
§§ Ibid. p. 11.

brought used during the trip to Indiana and after their arrival.[†]

It was in Indiana that Lincoln grew from a boy of seven years of age to a man. It was also in Indiana that Lincoln became acquainted with death and the profound grief and sorrow that accompanied it. Here he buried his mother, his sister, and his sister's newborn baby boy.

Lincoln was young, but large for his age, when his family became the twenty-eighth one to move into the Little Pigeon Creek Community. He worked from dawn to dusk helping his family establish their farm. The Lincolns kept chickens, hogs, oxen, a cow, horses, and sheep. Almost immediately, after moving to Indiana, an ax was put into young Abraham's hands. It was a useful tool in the wilderness, and for the next fourteen years, the young man was seldom without it.

The corn on the Lincolns' Indiana farm grew to amazing heights. A little over a mile from the their home was Noah Gordon's "horse mill," where young Abraham would take shelled corn to be ground into cornmeal—a staple in the pioneer family's diet. Other staples included pork, sorghum or maple syrup, and milk from their cow. Nancy's vegetable garden grew a variety of crops including potatoes, turnips, cabbage, beets, roasting ears, pumpkins, and squash. They also cultivated some fruits, as one story tells of Thomas catching a few neighbor boys raiding the Lincoln melon patch.[††]

In addition to fruit planted by the family, the woods of southern Indiana offered a wide range of wild fruits. An abundant of wild strawberries caused one traveler to comment "his horse's hoofs were red with their juice." During the summer months, the Lincoln

---

[†] Warren, *Lincoln's Youth*, p. 23.
[††] Ibid.

children searched for Juneberries, mulberries, black dewberries, blackberries, and red raspberries. In the fall, they searched for wild grapes, plums, crab apples, persimmons, and paw paws. These fruits were eaten fresh and baked into pies and cobblers. Others were dried or made into jams and jellies for winter consumption.[†††]

Rail Splitters

1	egg
3	tablespoons sugar
1	teaspoon salt
1	cup yellow corn meal
4	tablespoons melted lard, shortening, or butter
1	cup fresh buttermilk
½	teaspoon baking soda
1	teaspoon cold water
1	cup flour
4	teaspoons baking powder

Grease and flour a corn-muffin pan. Preheat over to 375 degrees.

Melt lard, shortening, or butter, and let cool a bit (it should not be hot.). Mix sugar, salt, and corn meal. Add beaten egg. Mix well. Slowly add melted fat. Mix again. Add buttermilk. Dissolve the baking soda in the 1 teaspoon of cold water. Add to mixture.

Sift flour and 4 teaspoons of baking powder together. Sift into batter.

Pour mixture into prepared muffin pan and bake about 15 minutes, or until golden brown.

---

††† Warren, *Lincoln's Youth*, p. 74.

When Thomas Lincoln moved to Indiana, he worked as a cask maker for a local man making applejack brandy.[§] Apples were a favorite among the pioneer families because they could be stored for a lengthy period of time, and because they were versatile. The oldest cookbooks and household books include recipes and instructions for drying apples for winter. Applesauce and apple butter were both made in large iron kettles, and usually cooked outdoors. It was recommended that applesauce be eaten with pork during the winter months as part of a healthy diet. Apples were stewed, baked, fried, sauced, and juiced. They were used in pies, tarts, dumplings, cobblers, and jellies. However, to most children, including the Lincoln children, a ripe apple fresh from the tree was a tasty treat. The green apples that the Lincolns enjoyed fried were the green or transparent apples which ripen in June. Granny Smith apples also are a suitable choice for frying. One should never use unripe fruit for cooking or eating at any time.

§ Conway, p. 11.

Fried Green Apples

2	tablespoons butter
1	cup sugar
	Cinnamon
3	to 4 green apples (peeled or unpeeled), sliced

Melt butter in a skillet over medium heat. (Note: If cooking over a fire, keep skillet near but not directlly over the flames. A few coals under a spider skillet are acceptable.) Drop in sliced green apples; sprinkle with sugar and cinnamon to taste. Cook slowly, stirring occasionally until apples are browned and tender.

Both the purplish roots and the green leaves of beets are edible, and both are high in vitamin C. It has been said that Lincoln "knew and tolerated" beets. Beets prepared in this method can be either refrigerated until ready to use, or sealed in sterilized jars in a 10-minute boiling-water bath.

Sweet Pickled Beets

Young beets
Boiling water
Sugar
Vinegar
Whole cloves

Peel small beets in a porcelain or enamel saucepan and add boiling water. Cook until beets are tender; set aside until cool.

Boil equal parts of sugar and vinegar along with ½ teaspoon cloves for every gallon of liquid used. Cloves should be tied in a cheesecloth bag. Pour sugar liquid over the beets. Allow to set until ready to use.

The Lincolns brought a few hogs and one cow when they moved to Indiana from Kentucky. Every fall, a hog was butchered to be used for the family's meat during the winter. Pork was a staple in Lincoln's diet.

Nancy's Pork Chops and Greens

6	thick pork chops
1	large clove garlic, minced
1	bay leaf
	Bit of flour
¼	cup water
¼	cup vinegar
	Salt and pepper
	Green vegetables of choice (cabbage, spinach, or green beans)

Season and flour pork chops. Brown them in hot fat. Add rest of ingredients and simmer until tender. Add more water if necessary. After meat is done, add green vegetables and cook in the liquid until tender.

Leaveners

In the 1790s, bakers found a way to make dough rise effectively. Potassium carbonate, commonly called pearlash, was widely used until the introduction of baking soda in 1840. Baking soda, or saleratus, was more effective, but required the addition of sour milk or cream of tartar to make dough rise sufficiently. This problem was solved in 1856 when baking soda and cream of tartar were combined and sold commercially. The new product was named baking powder, and with its introduction on the market, cooks saved hours of beating eggs and batter. Yeast, the most effective dough rising product, became commercially available sometimes around 1868. There were recipes for homemade yeast prior to this date, and it was indeed frequently made at home. Without a doubt, the commercial production of yeast made life a bit easier for the post-Civil War baker.

Gingerbread

Lincoln often told this story involving gingerbread men:

Once in a while my mother used to get some sorghum and some ginger and mix us up a batch of gingerbread. It wasn't often, and it was our biggest treat. One day I smelled it and came into the house to get my share while it was hot. I found she had baked me three gingerbread men, and I took them out under a hickory tree to eat them.

There was a family near us that was a little poorer than we were, and their boy came along as I sat down.

"Abe," he said, edging close, "gimme a man."

I gave him one. He crammed it into his mouth at two bites and looked at me while I bit the legs from my first one.

"Abe," he said, "gimme that other'n."

I wanted it, but I gave it to him, and as it followed the first one I said, "You seem to like gingerbread."

"Abe," he said earnestly, "I don't s'pose there's anybody on this earth likes gingerbread as well as I do," — and drawing a sigh that brought up crumbs — "an' I don't s'pose there's anybody gets less of it."

Young Abe's Gingerbread Men

1 cup butter
½ cup dark molasses or sorghum
1 cup sugar
1 teaspoon cinnamon
1 teaspoon ginger
1 teaspoon nutmeg
1 teaspoon cloves
2 eggs, well beaten
1 teaspoon vinegar
5 cups flour
1 teaspoon baking soda

Cream butter and sugar together. Add molasses, cinnamon, nutmeg, ginger, and cloves. Mix well. Pour into a saucepan. Bring to a boil, stirring constantly. As the mixture reaches the boiling point, remove from heat. Cool to lukewarm. Add eggs and vinegar; mix well. Sift together flour and baking soda; add to egg mixture. Mix again until mixture forms a smooth dough. Cover or wrap dough and place in a cool place (or in a refrigerator) for several hours or overnight.

When ready to bake, roll out on floured board. Cut with gingerbread-man or other shaped cutter. Raisins or other pieces of dried fruit can be used to decorate. Bake in preheated 350 degree oven on an ungreased cookie sheet for 8–10 minutes for four-inch cookies, or 6–7 minutes for one-inch cookies.

If preferred, cookies can be decorated with frosting after they have cooled.

Just as Lincoln enjoyed sorghum, so will anyone who tries this cake-like gingerbread.

Hot Water Sorghum Gingerbread

⅓ cup shortening
⅔ cup boiling water
1 cup sorghum
1 egg, well beaten
2 ¾ cups flour
2 teaspoons baking soda
1 teaspoon salt
1 ½ teaspoons ground ginger
1 teaspoon cinnamon
¼ teaspoon cloves

Grease and flour a 9 by 9-inch baking pan. Preheat oven to 350 degrees.

Melt shortening in boiling water. Remove from heat and let cool a bit. (If water is too hot, the egg will cook instead of blend.) Add sorghum and beaten egg. Sift dry ingredients together. Add to sorghum mixture and mix thoroughly. Pour batter into prepared pan and bake for 30 minutes.

Serve with whipped cream or ice cream.

For decades, this recipe was common throughout the United States before Sarah Hale published it in 1841.

Common Gingerbread

(Historic version)

Take a pound and a half of flour, and rub into it half a pound of butter; add half a pound of brown sugar and half a pint of molasses, two table-spoonfuls of cream, a teaspoonful of pearlash, and ginger to the taste. Make it into a stiff paste, and roll it out thin. Put it on buttered tins, and bake in a moderate oven.

Above: This replica of the Lincoln cabin stands in the Lincoln Pioneer Village in Rockport, Indiana.

Right: Large fireplaces such as this are similar to those the Lincoln family used when he was a boy. They featured substantial hearths with space for at least one Dutch oven for cooking and keeping family meals warm.

Both photos, author's collection.

Sweeteners

In pioneer America, sugar was not always readily available. Many homes contained sugar chests which could be locked, and the lady of the house, or a trusted servant, kept the key on her person. At times, sugar sold for as much as five dollars per pound. For cooks such as Nancy Lincoln, and later Sally Lincoln, alternatives were a necessity.

Molasses is a thick, rich, syrup separated from raw sugar during the refining process. There are four types of molasses, and all are high in calcium and iron. Light molasses has the mildest taste; dark molasses is heavier and less sweet; blackstrap molasses is a bitter waste product of sugar manufacturing and should not be used in baking; unsulphured molasses contains no sulphur dioxide and is specially manufactured from the juice of sun-ripened sugar cane.

Maple syrup is made from the sweet thick sap of maple trees.

Honey is a sweet, thick syrup made by honey bees. It is a nutritious sweetener which aides in the digestion process and contains iron, riboflavin, and Vitamin C. Generally, the lighter the honey in color, the more flavorful it is. Darker honey tends to have a stronger taste and should not be used in baking. When honey is used in cakes and breads, their keeping quality is enhanced. By using a slightly higher temperature, honey can be substituted for sugar in jams, jellies, and candies. To substitute honey used the following guidelines:

For breads, rolls, and general cooking, 1 cup of honey equals 1 cup of sugar.

For cakes and cookies, ⅞ cup of honey equals 1 cup of sugar.

In all other recipes, reduce any other liquid specified in a recipe by 3 tablespoons for each cup of honey substituted.

Sorghum is a dark syrup made from the sweet juices of the sorghum plant. It can be used in recipes which would normally call for molasses, but do not use it in jams or jellies. Sorghum has a unique flavor of its own, and it is also a wonderful condiment on fresh-baked breads and biscuits.

Honey and Almond Cake

½   cup shortening
½   teaspoon salt
½   teaspoon ginger
½   teaspoon cinnamon
1 ¼ cups honey
2   eggs
1   cup blanched, chopped
      almonds
2 ½ cups sifted cake flour
¼   teaspoon baking soda
1   teaspoon baking powder
½   cup water

Preheat oven to 325 degrees. Grease and flour a 9 by 9-inch baking pan.

Cream together shortening, salt, ginger, and cinnamon. Add 1 cup of the honey and mix till well blended. Beat in eggs one at a time.

Combine cake flour, baking soda, and baking powder; add to shortening and honey mixture alternately with water, blending well but not overbeating. Pour into prepared baking pan. Mix remaining honey with almonds and sprinkle over the top of the batter. (Do not pile them too high in one spot; this will cause the cake to collapse.) Bake for 60 minutes, or until cake tests done.

(NOTE: To blanch almonds, drop them in boiling water for a few seconds, then plunge them into cold water. The brown skins will then slip off easily. Almonds are easier to chop while they are still slightly damp.)

Milk sickness came to Indiana in the fall of 1818. This fatal disease was caused by an innocent-looking white wildflower commonly called snakeroot. As other vegetation died in the sweltering heat during a humid summer, snakeroot flourished. The cows would eat it, become sick, tremble, and die. People who drank milk from an infected cow were likely to take to their beds, fall into a coma, and die as well.

Many members of the Little Pigeon Creek Community fell victim to this illness. Nancy Lincoln's uncle Tom Sparrow and his wife Elizabeth both died leaving their nephew, Dennis Hanks, to live with the Lincoln family.[§] Nancy helped tend her sick relatives. Thomas Lincoln made the coffins, and young Abraham made the pegs which held the coffins together. On October 5, 1818, Nancy fell victim to milk sickness and succumbed. Her husband made her coffin, and her son whittled the pegs. She was buried on a knoll a quarter of a mile from the Lincoln cabin, and near the graves of her uncle and aunt.

In late November of the following year, Thomas Lincoln traveled to Elizabethtown, Kentucky. There, on December 2, he married Sally Bush Johnston, a widow with three children. The Lincoln cabin became crowded as there were now eight people living in it: Thomas, his new wife, his children Sarah and Abraham, Dennis Hanks, and Sally's three children: Elizabeth, John D., and Matilda. Sally brought a few belongings with her, including a bureau, a table, a clothespress, bedclothes, and kitchenware. But what Abraham was most interested in were the four books Sally brought—*Webster's Speller*, *Robinson Crusoe*, *The Arabian Nights*, and *Lessons in Elocution* by William Scott.[§§]

---

§ Warren, p. 53.

§§ Conway, p. 57.

This cooked cornmeal mixture is also known as mush.

Sally Johnston's Hasty Pudding

4   cups water
1   cup yellow or white
      cornmeal
1   teaspoon salt

Bring three cups of water to a boil in a saucepan.

Mix cornmeal and salt with the remaining 1 cup of cold water. Mix well. Slowly pour the mixture into the boiling water, stirring all the while. Cook until thickened, stirring often. Cover and continue to cook over very low heat for another 10 minutes. Serve hot.

Left-over pudding can be poured into a baking dish and stored in the refrigerator. It can then be sliced and fried in bacon drippings and eaten crisp.

Abraham Lincoln is my nam[e]
     And with my pen I wrote the same[.]
I wrote in both hast[e] and speed
     and left it here for fools to read.

                — Abraham Lincoln

For special dinners, feast, or celebrations, women would gather edible flower petals and leaves such as those from roses, pansies, borage, and wild mint. These were then used in teas, or candied to be eaten as a unique treat or used as an edible decoration for other foods.

Candied Mint Leaves

Fresh mint leaves or
    flower petals
Egg whites
Sugar (either powdered or
    granulated)

Wash the leaves and petals carefully. Dry on a towel, keeping them unbroken. Dip each one into unbeaten egg whites. Press into the sugar and spread out on a board to dry. Shake off excess sugar. Place in the refrigerator to harden.

Sprinkle in a salad, on top of fruit, on top of a cake, in a punch bowl, or eat like candy.

Abraham Lincoln,
His hand and pen.
He will be good,
But God knows when.

On August 4, 1826, Sarah Lincoln married Aaron Grigsby, the eldest son of Reuben Grigsby. To commemorate his sister's wedding, young Abraham recited a poem at the reception. While some attribute the poem to Abraham, most doubt that he is the author. Versions of it were printed as early as the 1780s.[§]

> *As Adam was resting in slumber*
> *He lost a short rib from his side.*
> *And when he awoke 'twas in wonder*
> *to see a most beautiful bride.*
>
> *The Lord then was not willing*
> *The man should be alone,*
> *But caused a sleep upon him*
> *And took from him a bone.*
>
> *The woman was not taken*
> *From Adam's feet we see,*
> *So he must not abuse her*
> *The meaning seems to be.*
>
> *This woman, she was taken*
> *From under Adam's arm.*
> *So she must be protected*
> *From injuries and harm.*

[§] Conway, p. 85; Warren, pp. 152 and 251.

Sarah Lincoln's Wedding Dinner[†]

Two fat wild turkeys roasted a rich brown

A saddle of deer meat

Six large vegetable pies, full of turnips, beans, and potatoes

A big bowl of wild honey

A bowl of maple sugar

At least a hundred fried Kentucky Wonders

Watermelon preserves

Cherry preserves

Bushel of pawpaws

Tea

[†] French, *Lincoln Heritage Trail Cookbook*, p.4.

Vegetable Pies

Pastry for double-crust
 pie
3 turnips
3 potatoes
2 cups green beans
1 onion
3 carrots
Other vegetables as
 desired (celery, corn,
 okra)
3 tablespoons butter
2 tablespoons flour
2 cups of chicken or turkey
 broth
1 teaspoon ground
 rosemary
Salt and pepper to taste
1 egg, beaten

Cut all vegetables into small chunks and set aside. In a large skillet, heat the butter until it bubbles. Sprinkle over with flour; stir until it forms a smooth paste. Gradually add the two cups of broth. Cook over medium heat, stirring constantly until thick and creamy. Add the cut vegetables and rosemary. Season to taste. Heat thoroughly.

Preheat oven to 350 degrees. Roll out half of the pastry and place it in a greased casserole dish, leaving a 1-inch overhang. Spoon the hot vegetable mixture into the pastry. Roll out remaining pastry and fit over filling. Trim and crimp crusts together. Slash steam vents in a decorative pattern on upper crust. Brush with beaten egg. Bake for 45–60 minutes or until crust is golden brown and vegetables are done.

Kentucky Wonders

3   tablespoons lard (or oil)
3   eggs
3   tablespoons sugar
     Sifted flour

Melt lard and allow to cool; add eggs and mix well. (If using oil, no need to heat.) Add sugar and beat mixture. Add enough sifted flour to make a dough (similar to pie dough).

Roll dough to about ⅛-inch thickness. Cut into squares three inches long and two inches wide. Cut several slits lengthwise to within a quarter of an inch of the edges of the pieces of dough. Run two forefingers through every other slit. Lay them down on the board lengthwise and dent them. Fry in hot lard or oil until a light brown.

This recipe works well for almost any fruit.

Cherry Preserves

Select large red cherries. Stem and stone them saving all of the juice. Weigh the fruit and add an equal amount of sugar. Sprinkle the sugar over the cherries and let them stand for at least six hours. Pour into a heavy-bottomed pan, adding the juices. Heat slowly, skimming the foam from mixture several times. Simmer until the cherries are clear, about 30–40 minutes. Cool and seal in jars. Store in a cool, dark place.

NOTE: Tiny new mint leaves may be shredded and added for a unique flavor.

Watermelon Preserves

11 cups watermelon rind
9 cups sugar
8 cups water
2 oranges, sliced
4 lemons, sliced
2 sticks cinnamon
4 teaspoons powdered
   cloves

Wash watermelon rinds. Peel the outer green skin, leaving the white portion of rind. Cut the rind into one-inch chunks. Place in a large saucepan or kettle with ½ cups salt to one gallon of water and soak for at least eight hours. Drain the salt water. Replace with fresh water and cook rind chunks until tender, about 30 minutes.

In another saucepan combine sugar, the 8 cups of water, orange and lemon slices, cinnamon sticks, and powdered cloves. Boil for five minutes. Add watermelon rind and cook until translucent.

Pour into hot sterilized jars and seal in a boiling water bath for 10 minutes.

On January 20, 1828, Abraham Lincoln's beloved sister, Sarah, died in childbirth. She was buried holding her baby boy in her arms in the Little Pigeon Creek Baptist Church Cemetery.[§]

The Lincoln family left Indiana in the spring of 1830. Abraham thought he might never go back to the Little Pigeon Creek Community again, but he did return years later.

Lincoln described his visit:

In the fall of 1844, thinking I might aid some to carry the State of Indiana for Mr. Clay, I went into the neighborhood in that State in which I was raised, where my mother and only sister were buried, and from which I had been absent about fifteen years. That part of the country is, within itself, as unpoetical as any spot of the earth; but still, seeing it and its objects and inhabitants aroused feelings in me which were certainly poetry; though whether my expression of these feelings is poetry is quite another question.[§§]

---

§ Conway, *Young Abe Lincoln: His Teenage Years in Indiana*, p. 94.

§§ Basler, *The Collected Works of Abraham Lincoln*, p.378

Upon returning to Indiana, and seeing his old friends and neighbors, Lincoln was inspired to write the following poem:

My Childhood's Home

My childhood's home I see again.
    And sadden with the view;
And still, as memory crowds my brain,
    There's pleasure in it too.

O Memory! thou midway world
    'Twixt earth and paradise,
Where things decayed and loved ones lost
    In dreamy shadows rise,

And, freed from all that's earthly vile,
    Seem hallowed, pure, and bright,
Like scenes in some enchanted isle
    All bathed in liquid light.

As dusky mountains please the eye
    When twilight chases day;
As bugle-notes that, passing by,
    In distance die away;

As leaving some grand waterfall,
    We, lingering, list its roar —
So memory will hallow all
    We've known, but know no more.

Near twenty years have passed away
    Since here I bid farewell
To woods and fields, and scenes of play,
    And playmates loved so well.

Where many were, but few remain
    Of old familiar things,
But seeing them, to mind again,
    The lost and absent brings.

The friends I left the parting day,
    How changed, as time has sped!
Young childhood grown, strong manhood gray,
    And half of all are dead.

I hear the loved survivors tell
    How nought from death could save,
Till every sound appears a knell,
    And every spot a grave.

I range the field with pensive tread
    And pace the hollow rooms,
And feel (companion of the dead)
    I'm living in the tombs.

1830 – 1861

The Lincoln Home in Springfield, Illinois.

Illustration by Amy Castleberry.

*A*fter saying good-bye at his mother's gravesite, Lincoln and his extended family were ready to leave the Little Pigeon Creek community to settle in Coles County, Illinois. On March 1, 1830, three wagons containing thirteen people pulled out of the area Lincoln had called home for fourteen years. He was then twenty-one years old.

Lincoln stayed with his family for about a year, helping them establish their new home. Then, in July 1831, Lincoln settled in New Salem, Illinois, a small thriving settlement. For a while he lived at the Rutledge Tavern and took most of his meals there. He sharpened his grammar skills and studied to become a lawyer. In New Salem the young man developed his interest in politics, and was twice elected as the district's representative to the state legislative body. He was part of what was knows as "The Long Nine," a group of men known for their height, who were instrumental in moving the Illinois state capital from Vandalia to Springfield.

Soon Lincoln found himself moving to Springfield. When he arrived, he stopped at the store belonging to Joshua Speed and inquired about the price of bedding. Upon realizing that Lincoln did not have enough money to purchase a bed, Joshua said that he had one and that Lincoln could live with him above the store. Beds were a luxury for many, and Lincoln considered himself fortunate to find a place to sleep. He carried his dusty saddlebags upstairs, and upon returning said, "Well, Speed, I am moved."

Lincoln became the junior law partner to John Todd Stuart, and through him became part of Springfield's social scene. Tall and awkward, Lincoln lacked many of the social graces which most women found attractive in a man. He was neither a handsome nor genteel man, but he did possess a quick mind and a keen sense of humor. No one could tell a story better than Abraham Lincoln. It was this quality that first caught the attention of Mary Ann Todd, a Kentucky belle who was residing in Springfield.

Mary's two older, married sisters, Elizabeth Edwards and Frances Wallace, both lived in Springfield. Elizabeth had married Ninian Edwards, the son of Illinois' only territorial governor. Frances had married William Wallace, a physician and pharmacist.

Mary was a five-foot three-inch, blue-eyed beauty who had received a remarkable education. She had come to Illinois from Lexington, Kentucky, to stay with her sister Elizabeth, who hoped Mary would find a suitable husband and make Springfield her permanent home. Possessing an infectious laugh and a quick wit, Mary looked intensely at people when they spoke, as if hanging onto their every word. Several men desired to be her dance partner, her escort, and a few desired to be her husband. They found her to be interesting, enthralling, and beautiful. Ninian Edwards best described Mary by stating, "[She] could make a bishop forget his prayers."[†]

Todd family legend indicates Mary met her candidate for the position of "suitable husband" at a party hosted by Elizabeth Edwards. Young Mr. Lincoln knew of this warm, cheery, and vivacious lass through John Todd Stuart, his law partner and Mary's first cousin. After the couple had been introduced, Lincoln boldly held out his hand, bowed slightly, and said, "Miss Todd, I wish to dance with you in the worst way." After a few turns across the dance floor with her awkward dance partner, Mary returned to the other young ladies and assured them that Lincoln had indeed danced in the worst way possible.

Despite that less than perfect first dance, the two began courting.

---

† Baker, *Mary Todd Lincoln: A Biography*, p. 79.

This portrait of Mary Lincoln was painted in 1925 by her niece Katherine Helm at the request of Robert Todd Lincoln. (Townsend Collection of Mary Genevieve Townsend Murphy)

Soon, they discovered their many common interests. They both enjoyed poetry, especially that of Scotland's noble bard, Robert Burns. They shared an interest in theatre, especially the plays of William Shakespeare. Often, the couple could be found in Elizabeth's parlor reading Shakespearean scenes to one another. Politically, they held the same views—they were both Whigs. Women could not yet vote, but that did not stop Mary from having political opinions. She had been raised in a political home where politics permeated the conversation, the entertainment, and the business of the household. Mary's father, Robert Smith Todd, was a supporter and friend to Henry Clay, a frequent guest in the Todd home. Lincoln admired Clay greatly. Lincoln and Mary soon found they had much in common.

To many, including Mary's sister Elizabeth, Lincoln and Mary were mismatched. He was tall and lanky; she was short and slightly round. He had been born and raised in frontier log cabins; she had been born and raised in stately brick mansions. He had lived in the backwoods and wilderness; she had lived in Lexington, Kentucky, the "Athens of the West." He had little schooling; Mary had received twelve years of formal education. Lincoln was in debt; Mary was the daughter of a wealthy businessman.

Despite their differences, the two were drawn together. Against all odds, and against her family's wishes, Mary and Abraham became a couple.

They did have a difficult courtship, and even broke their engagement sometime around the first of January 1841. After months of separation, friends, Mr. and Mrs. Simeon Francis, held a dinner party that brought the two together again. They courted in secret without telling Mary's sister. Finally, they separately told Ninian and Elizabeth that they planned to marry. Elizabeth was livid. The room was filled with words such as "plebeian" and "white trash."

Mary, quite the dramatic woman herself, held her ground. She would marry Mr. Lincoln! Eventually, Ninian intervened and made Elizabeth realize the wedding was going to take place and it would take place in their home. Elizabeth snapped that she did not have time to bake a proper wedding cake, and she would have to send out for gingerbread and beer. Mary retorted that would be good enough for "plebeians." Invitations were quickly sent to a select few relatives and friends. Frances came to help Elizabeth make preparations. She later commented that she had never worked harder in her life than on Mary's wedding day. The two sisters joined forces, and Mary did have a proper wedding cake—it was still warm when she and Abraham sliced it.[††]

Abraham Lincoln in 1860.
(Courtesy Abe's Antiques of Gettysburg)

Mary Lincoln about 1846.
(Author's collection)

†† Randall, *Biography of a Marriage*, page 72.

Afterward, the newlyweds lived in a four-dollar-per-week boarding room at the Globe Tavern. Many have discussed the humbleness of the Lincolns' beginnings there, although in fact, the Globe was a respectable, middle-class, boarding house where many young married couples first took up residence, including Mary's sister Frances and her husband William Wallace, and cousin John Todd Stuart and his wife.

Soon after the birth of their first son, Robert, the Lincolns moved to a rented cottage and then purchased a home on the corner of Eighth and Jackson streets. They lived there for the next seventeen years, and the family grew as three more boys were born. Mary was a doting mother; Lincoln was a permissive father. In an era when children's birthdays were seldom celebrated, Mary held birthday parties for her sons, sometimes inviting as many as fifty other children.[†††]

Much has been said about the Lincoln marriage. Mary was quick-tempered, feisty, and given to emotional mood swings. Abraham was often melancholy, a workaholic, and occasionally absent from the home for months at a time. They were truly opposites in many ways. Separately, they were both highly sensitive and emotionally unstable. But together they shared a deep, profound love that only the two of them completely understood. He was her "Mr. Lincoln" and she was his "Molly."

---

††† Ibid. p. 100.

In the summer of 1851, the Lincoln family traveled to Kentucky to visit the Todd family and to settle the estate of Mary's father. Mary sat with a notebook and pencil and tried to take directions of a "pinch of this, a little of that, and sweeten to taste" from Chaney, the family cook, who was distressed because Mary had no one to make beaten biscuits and corn bread for her.[§] The recipe below appears as Mary would have used it.

Beaten Biscuits[§§]
(Historic version)

1	pint of flour
1	rounded tablespoon of lard
1	good pinch of salt
	Sweet milk

Mix with very cold sweet milk to a stiff dough. Work 150 times through a kneader, or beat with a hammer for half an hour. Roll into sheet one-half inch thick. Cut out or make out with the hands. Stick with a fork and bake in a hot oven about twenty minutes till a rich brown. Be careful not to have the oven too hot or it will blister the biscuits.

BEATEN-BISCUIT SUGGESTIONS

The dough can be kept for two days if put in a tightly covered jar and kept on ice or in a cool place. Roll from 150 to 200 times through the kneader. Bake from twenty to twenty-five minutes in a hot oven. If the stove is hot enough to blister them before they are baked, place a bread-pan on the upper grating. Many of the best housekeepers prefer the old way of making the biscuits out by hand to the use of the cutter.

---

§ Helm, *Mary Wife of Lincoln*, p. 103.
§§ Fox, *The Blue Grass Cookbook*, p. 1.

Beaten Biscuits

(Modern version)

8	cups sifted flour
¼	teaspoon soda
½	teaspoon sugar
¾	cup lard
1	teaspoon salt
1	cup water

Sift dry ingredients together. Cut in lard until the consistency of fine meal. Stir in 1 cup water; blend thoroughly. Place dough on a wooden block; turn frequently and pound with a hammer for 20–30 minutes until the dough blisters and becomes satiny in texture.

Roll dough to ½-inch thickness; cut with a small biscuit cutter. Bake in preheated oven at 400 degrees for 25 minutes or until lightly browned.

Golden Corn Bread

1	cup corn meal
1	cup flour
¼	cup sugar
4	teaspoons baking powder
1	teaspoon salt
1	egg
1	cup milk
4	tablespoons butter

Melt butter in an iron skillet. Mix together all dry ingredients. Stir in egg and slowly add milk. Add melted butter from skillet, making sure that the entire bottom of the skillet is coated with butter. Mix batter well. Pour into hot iron skillet and bake in oven at 375 for 20–25 minutes.

In addition to beaten biscuits and corn bread, later in her life, Mary missed other foods from her youth and married life in Springfield. While living in France, she wrote to her grandnephew, Louis Baker (grandson of Elizabeth Edwards):

"How I long to see you all—to have a taste of your dear Grandma's good food—waffles, batter cakes, egg corn bread—are all unknown here—as to biscuits, light rolls && they have never been dreamed of—not to speak of buckwheat cakes."[†]

Biscuits

(Historic version)

1	quart flour,
1	pint of buttermilk,
1	tablespoon lard,
½	teaspoon soda,
½	teaspoon salt,

Make into biscuits and bake quickly.

NOTE: Modern cooks can achieve the same results by substituting a healthier shortening for the lard.

In July of 1840, McConnel, Bunn & Co. opened for business in Springfield. Two years later, Jacob Bunn bought the business and operated it as a wholesale and retail grocery store and changed the name to J. Bunn & Co. According to their 1849–1850 ledger, Mary Lincoln purchased some of the family's grocery staples, including sugar and coffee, from the store. (Jacob Bunn Ledger, 1849)

[†] Turner, *Mary Todd Lincoln: Her Life and Letters*, p. 690.

Light Rolls

4 ½ teaspoons active dry yeast

½ cup warm water (110° to 115°)

2 cups warm milk (110° to 115°)

6 tablespoons shortening

2 eggs

¼ cup sugar

1 ½ teaspoons salt

7 to 7 ½ cups all-purpose flour

In a large mixing bowl, dissolve yeast in warm water. Add the milk, shortening, eggs, sugar, salt and 3 cups flour; beat until smooth. Stir in enough remaining flour to form a soft dough.

Turn onto a floured surface; knead until smooth and elastic, about 6–8 minutes (dough will be sticky). Place in a greased bowl, turning once to grease top. Cover and let rise in a warm place until doubled, about 1 hour.

Punch dough down. Turn onto a lightly floured surface; divide into 24 pieces. Shape each into a roll. Place 2 inches apart on greased baking sheets. Cover and let rise until doubled, about 30 minutes. Bake at 350 degrees for 20–25 minutes or until golden brown. Serve warm. Yield: 2 dozen.

Batter Cakes

(Historic version)

Sift together ½ cup each of flour and cornmeal with a pinch of salt, then scald with boiling water. Stir until smooth.

Beat 2 eggs well and add to mixture. Thin the batter with about half a pint of sweet milk.

Drop by spoonfuls on a hot, well-greased griddle. The batter must run freely. Serve hot. These are good with butter, honey, or maple syrup for breakfast.

Southern Waffles

(Historic version)

1   pint flour
1   pint buttermilk
1   egg
½   teaspoon baking soda
       dissolved in a little
       water
1   teaspoon sugar
1   teaspoon salt
1   teaspoon baking powder
1   tablespoon corn meal
1   tablespoon melted butter

Mix all ingredients together thoroughly. Pour batter into a waffle pan and bake over medium coals. Flip and bake on the other side.

NOTE: Modern cooks will probably want to use a waffle iron instead of a waffle pan. The modern waffle iron cooks the batter on both sides at the same time and there is no need to flip the pan.

Basic Waffles

2   cups sifted flour
3   teaspoons baking powder
1   tablespoon sugar
½   teaspoon salt
3   eggs, separated
1 ½   cups milk
5   tablespoons melted
       shortening

Mix and sift dry ingredients. Combine beaten egg yolks, milk and shortening; add to dry ingredients, beating until smooth. Fold in stiffly beaten egg whites. Pour batter into each section of a hot waffle iron.

Photo # b5β4p2 courtesy of Lincoln Home National Historic Site, Springfield, Illinois.

The Lincolns depended upon wood-burning stoves to make their batter cakes and waffles. The one shown above is a cast-iron Royal Oak Number 9, is the second stove the Lincolns purchased. Manufactured by Jewett and Root of Buffalo, New York, it is a wood-burner with four lids and a wide hearth. Used by the family prior to their departure for Washington, it is still in good, serviceable condition.

The stove was purchased from dealer Eli Kreigh in Springfield on June 9, 1860, just after the primary election. Because they would be entertaining more, Mary decided they needed a better and larger model than the one she had, thus precipitating the purchase of this one.

The nursery in the Todd home (*above*) held a variety of dolls, toys, and small furnishings to delight the children of the family, and gave them a place to play away from the elegant furnishings throughout the rest of the house. The room also contained a trundle bed that could hold up to nine small children if they slept across it horizontally.

(Photos this page and facing page: author's collection.)

Nineteenth-century housekeepers stored valuable sugar in a special chest that could be locked, such as this one (right). The key was kept by the mistress of the house or a trusted servant.

When Abraham Lincoln met his wife's family for the first time at the Todd home in Lexington, they stood in the great hall in hierarchical order—Papa, Mama, children, and servants—to meet their new son-in-law and welcome Mary home again.

The dining room in the Todd home.

During the seventeenth and eighteenth century, homes such the Todds' in Lexington often had a kitchen separate from the main house, used during the summer months to avoid heating the main house and to reduce risk of fire. The Todds' meals were cooked in the summer kitchen by servants and brought inside to the warming kitchen. There, food was kept warm in the ovens and on the hearth until time to serve the meal.

(All photos, author's collection.)

In early 1861, a young J. W. Watson came to visit President Lincoln to discuss his future in the military. During their talk, a man entered the office carrying "two cups and saucers, a plain tin pot, and the usual paraphernalia for tea or coffee." † *Lincoln graciously invited Mr. Watson to join him for refreshments. During the break, their conversation turned to a discussion as to whether the actual coffee bean, or the making of it, produces a better beverage. Lincoln related a story of "traveling all night, cramped up in a stage, in southern Illinois" when he was a young man. When the stage stopped for breakfast at a small inn, Lincoln dined on "fried chicken, buckwheat cakes, and coffee." He told Watson, "Such coffee, sir! To say nothing of the buckwheat cakes and chicken, I had never before tasted. It was delicious, and as I found out afterward was simply made from parched rye."* ††

Buckwheat Cakes

(Historic version)

NOTE: *Indian meal is a coarse-ground cornmeal.*

Take one quart buckwheat meal, a handful of Indian meal, and a teaspoon of salt. Mix them with two large spoonfuls of yeast and sufficient cold water to make a thick batter. Put in a warm place to rise, which will take up to four hours. If you mix the batter the night before, let it stand where it is rather cool.

When it is light, bake it on a griddle or in a pan. The griddle must be well buttered, and the cakes are better to be small and thin.

---

† Watson J. W. "With Four Great Men." *North American Review*, Vol. 147, No. 5., p. 590.

†† Ibid.

Buckwheat Cakes

(Modern version)

1   cup sifted buckwheat
       flour
1   teaspoon baking powder
1 ½ tablespoons sugar
¼   teaspoon soda
¼   teaspoon salt
1   egg, well beaten
1   cup sour milk
1   tablespoon melted butter

Combine sifted flour, baking powder, sugar, salt, and soda; sift again. Combine milk and beaten egg; add to the flour. Stir just until smooth. Add melted butter.

Bake on a hot griddle, turning when edges are done. Serve hot with maple syrup, molasses, sorghum, or honey.

Mary purchased a copy of *Miss Leslie's Cookery* and a copy of *Miss Leslie's House Book or Manual of Domestic Economy for Town and Country* from Corneau & Diller in Springfield. (Hickey, "Lincolniana: The Lincoln Account at the Corneau and Diller Drug Store 1849–1861," pp. 60–61.)

Fricasseed Chicken

2 to 3 fryers, cut up
  Salt and pepper to taste
  Flour for dredging
  Lard or shortening
½ pint cream
¼ teaspoon nutmeg
¼ teaspoon mace
1 small piece of butter,
   rolled in a little flour
  Parsley sprigs

Cut chickens into pieces. Wipe pieces dry, season with salt and pepper, and dredge lightly with flour. Melt lard or shortening in frying pan, add chicken and fry until brown on all sides. When done, transfer to a covered pan and keep warm.

Skim the drippings in the frying pan, and add the cream. Season with nutmeg, mace, salt, and pepper. Thicken gravy with the small bit of butter rolled in flour. Stir carefully to be sure that the mixture is smooth. Bring to a good boil, then pour it over the hot chicken. Add a little more lard or butter into the frying pan. Fry the parsley sprigs but keep it green and crisp. Garnish the chicken with parsley.

❧

According to Isaac Arnold: "Mrs. Lincoln's table was famed for the excellence of many rare Kentucky dishes, and in season, it was loaded with venison, wild turkeys, prairie chickens, quail and other game, which was then abundant." §

---

§ From an address Arnold gave before the Illinois State Bar Association in Springfield on January 7, 1881. *History of Sangamon County*, Illinois, p. 86.

During his presidency, Lincoln often became weary and ill from irregular eating habits. Mary, concerned for her husband's heath, would send or take trays of food to his office. Often the tray was left untouched because he was too distracted to eat. Knowing his favorite foods, Mary asked a servant, Alice Johnstone, if she knew how to "make a dish of fricasseed chicken and small biscuits with thick cream gravy poured over it, all on one platter." When Alice replied that she would try, a plan was devised to have a home-style dinner in the small dining room with only family in attendance. Tad was sent to coax his father to dinner. When Lincoln entered the room, he replied, "Oh, Mary, this is good. It seems like old times come back!" It was reported that Lincoln ate and laughed heartily that evening. Later Tad reported to Alice that their plan had been a success for Lincoln "ate three helps and more gravy than you and me and mother could!" †

White Fricassee of Chicken

2 to 3 fryers, cut up
Salt and pepper to taste
¼ teaspoon nutmeg
¼ teaspoon mace
Sweet marjoram
½ pint cream
A bit of butter rolled in flour
Small forcemeat balls (optional)

Cut chickens into desired pieces and remove skin. Season with salt, pepper, nutmeg, and mace. Sprinkle some shredded marjoram over the chicken. Put all into a stew pot, and pour in the cream or whole milk. Add butter rolled in flour, and if you choose, the forcemeat balls. Set the stew pan over a low flame. Keep it tightly covered, and stew or simmer gently until the chicken is quite tender, but do not allow to boil. Serve hot.

(* Forcemeat is finely chopped, highly seasoned meat mixed with bread crumbs, similar to sausage.)

---

† Randall, *Biography of a Marriage*, p. 339.

Butter-Browned Steak with Coffee-Mustard Sauce

4	club, shell, or strip steaks cut 1-inch thick
2	tablespoons butter
	Salt and pepper to season
4	teaspoons spicy prepared mustard
⅔	cup strong hot coffee

In a very large, heavy, skillet, melt butter. Place steaks in skillet and brown quickly on both sides. For a rare steak, remove to a hot platter and keep warm. For a medium-rare or medium steak, turn the heat under the skillet to low and let the steaks cook slowly for 5–8 minutes longer. (Cook longer for a well-done steak.)

Remove steaks to a platter. Sprinkle steaks with salt and pepper. Spread 1 teaspoon of mustard on each steak. Pour coffee into the skillet and quickly bring to a simmer, scraping up the browned bits on the bottom of the skillet. Pour over steaks and serve.

Broiled Beefsteak

¾	pound of meat and bone per person
	Salt and pepper
	Butter
	English mustard

Trim excess fat from meat. Rinse and wipe the steak dry. Place in a broiling pan on a hot broiling rack about 3 inches from the heat source. When steak becomes browned, turn with two spoons to prevent piercing the meat. Broil for 10 more minutes for rare meat, longer for well-done meat. Place steak on a hot platter. Season with salt and pepper. Dot with butter. Skim off the fat from the drippings and pour the juice over the meat. Serve hot with English mustard.

Oysters

Enjoyed during times of celebration, such as weddings, Fresh oysters were a delicacy in the nineteenth century just as they are today. Transportation problems—slow river traffic, lack of railroads in some areas and poor road conditions in others—made transporting shellfish of any kind difficult; thus, in the early part of the nineteenth century, oysters were enjoyed only by the wealthy.

Oysters had to arrive at their destination within two weeks of harvesting to be considered "fresh." For longer journeys, they were often pickled prior to shipment. As the railroad industry expanded across America, bringing with it the ability to transport goods to the far-reaching communities on the western frontier, the prospect of having fresh oysters became more feasible. Indeed, one company even ran an "oyster line," priding itself on its ability to deliver oysters and other shellfish fresh from the eastern seacoast to Pittsburg.

Oysters probably continued their journey through the region by riverboat or by refrigerated train cars. They were shipped from New Orleans to St. Louis to Illinois by way of riverboat, then by train or stagecoach to various nearby communities. Oral tradition claims that the oysters' freshness on these journeys may have been ensured by being placed in baskets or nets, hung over the sides of the boats, and kept in the cool river water.

Because of their sensitivity to heat and humidity, oysters were harvested during the fall, winter, and early spring. The sage advice to eat oysters only during months containing the letter "r" stood as a reminder that only during those cooler months of the year did the temperature allow oysters to be safely shipped.

So in February 1837, when a group of politicians called the Long

Nine had much to celebrate, fresh oysters were available. For weeks these men had campaigned to have the Illinois State Capitol moved from Vandalia to Springfield. Promises were made; deals were drafted, and the vote was cast. The legislature voted to move its business north to Springfield. That evening, all of the legislatures were invited to Capp's Tavern for a victory celebration. Ninian Edwards paid the total bill of $223.50 for "cigars, oysters, almonds, and raisins."[†] No mention was made of how the oysters were prepared.

† Donald, David Herbert, *Lincoln*. New York: Simon & Schuster, 1995. p. 64.

Scalloped Oysters

(NOTE: Never have more than a double layer of oysters in this dish or the middle will not bake.)

1	pint of oysters
2	tablespoons light cream
½	cup day-old bread crumbs
1	cup cracker crumbs
½	cup melted butter
	Salt and freshly ground pepper
	Paprika

Preheat oven to 425 degrees. Drain oysters, reserving ¼ cup of the liquid. Combine oyster liquid and cream; set aside. Mix both kinds of crumbs together; add melted butter. Sprinkle a thick layer of crumbs in a 1-quart casserole dish. Cover with half of the oysters, followed by half of the cream mixture. Sprinkle lightly with salt and pepper. Cover with the second layer of crumbs, then oysters, then cream. Add more salt and pepper. Cover with remaining crumbs. Sprinkle with paprika. Bake for 30 minutes.

In December 1855, several of the Todd family members including Mary Lincoln attended the wedding of Caroline Lamb and William J. Black. In a letter to his daughter Elizabeth, John Todd Stuart wrote of the wedding meal which began with oyster salad and ended with ice cream and cake.[†]

Oyster Salad

This historic version calls for the cook to make her own mayonnaise.

1	quart oysters, cut—not chopped—into small pieces
1	bunch celery, cut—not chopped—into small pieces
2	hard-boiled eggs
2	raw eggs, well whipped
1	great spoonful salad oil
1	teaspoonful powdered sugar
1	small spoonful salt
1	small spoonful pepper
1	small spoonful made mustard
½	cup best cider vinegar

Drain the liquor well from the oysters and dice them with a sharp knife. Cut the celery, which should be white and crisp, into pieces of corresponding size. Set them aside in separate vessels, in a cold place while you prepare the dressing. Beat the eggs light (with a "Dover" egg-beater, if you have one), mix in the sugar; then whip in gradually the oil until it is a light cream.

Have ready, rubbed to a powder, the boiled yolks; add to them the salt, pepper, and lastly the mustard. Beat these into the oil and yolk, and then, two or three drops at a time, the vinegar, whipping the dressing briskly, but lightly for two or three minutes. It should, if properly managed, be like rich yellow cream, or custard.

With a silver fork, toss up the oysters and celery together in a glass dish; pour half of the dressing over them; toss up—not stir it down—for a minute, and pour the rest on the top.

---

† Pratt, *The Personal Finances of Abraham Lincoln*, p. 96.

Lay a border of light-green celery tufts close within the edge of the bowl, with a cluster in the middle of the salad. Serve as soon as may be, after it is mixed. Meanwhile, keep on the ice.

Oyster Salad

(Modern Version)

Oysters in their own liquor
Celery
Capers
Mayonnaise
Lettuce

Cook the oysters in their own liquor allowing them to boil up. Place on a platter and place in refrigerator allowing them to get ice cold. Cut up into small pieces—do not chop.

Cut up bits of crisp celery and mix with ½ cup capers. Add mayonnaise. Serve with lettuce.

Oyster Pie

1	tablespoon butter
2	onions, chopped
1	rib celery, chopped
3	tablespoons butter
3	tablespoons flour
1	cup milk
½	cup of oyster liquor
	Dash of mace
	Dash of thyme
	Pinch of minced parsley
1	pint of oysters
	Sherry
	Pastry for 2-crust pie

Melt the 1 tablespoon butter, add the onion and celery and cook until tender. Add the 3 tablespoons of butter and the 3 tablespoons of flour. Mix well. Add milk and oyster liquor. Add spices. Add oysters. Cook until the edges of the oysters curl. Add just enough sherry to thin the sauce. Stir.

Preheat oven to 375 degrees. Pour oyster mixture into a pastry shell and cover with remaining pastry. Bake for 40–50 minutes until browned

Steamed Oysters

1	quart of oysters
	Salt and pepper to taste
	Butter

Drain oysters and place in a shallow baking dish. Put the pan into a steamer over boiling water. Steam the oysters until they become plump with curled edges. Do not overcook. Transfer the oysters to a heated serving dish. Dot with butter. Season with salt and pepper to taste. Serve immediately.

Steamed Oysters in the Shell

Wash and scrub the oysters and place them in a pan or casserole with tight-fitting lid. The upper shells must be facing downward to prevent the oyster liquor from running out when the shells open.

Place the pan or casserole over a kettle of rapidly boiling water and steam until the shells open, about 10 minutes.

The *Illinois Journal* reported on January 31, 1855, that the Ladies of the First Presbyterian Church were scheduled to hold a repast on February 16 "where lovers of hot coffee, meats, jellies, oyester, &c., can be amply served at nine o'clock."

The ladies of New Salem remembered that Lincoln was fond of their fruit pies. After he was elected President, they would bake pies and ship them to him in Washington. Often, they would vent the pie by shaping a letter into the crust for what type of pie it was. An "A" represented an apple pie, "G" was a gooseberry. Sometimes, the pie was vented with the letter "L" for Lincoln.

New Salem Fruit Pies

Pastry for a double-crust
    9-inch pie
1 ½ tablespoon flour
1   cup sugar
¼   teaspoon salt
1   quart of fruit of choice
    (apples, blueberries,
    gooseberries, or
    cherries)

Preheat oven to 450 degrees. Line the pie plate with the unbaked pie crust. Place fruit in the pie shell. Mix together sugar, flour, and salt and pour over fruit. Place top crust over filling; crimp edges and cut gashes in top crust to allow steam to escape. Bake for 10 minutes. Reduce temperature to 350 degrees and bake for another 25–30 minutes.

(Note: If the fruit is tart, such as sour cherries, the sugar content may need to be increased slightly; if the fruit is extremely juicy, such as blackberries, the sugar content may need to be lessened slightly.)

When Lincoln lived in New Salem, Illinois, he was known to eat many of his meals at the Rutledge Tavern. This pie was a favorite.

Rutledge Tavern Squash Pie

1   unbaked 9-inch pie shell
1   egg, separated
2   whole eggs
2   cups milk
2   cups cooked, mashed squash
½   teaspoon salt
¼   cup brown sugar
1   tablespoon melted butter
1   teaspoon cinnamon
¼   teaspoon nutmeg
¼   teaspoon ginger

Preheat oven to 450 degrees. Lightly beat the egg white and brush the crust lightly with it. Beat the 2 whole eggs and the 1 egg yolk with milk and squash. Add salt, brown sugar, butter, and spices. Mix together thoroughly.

Pour mixture into prepared pie shell. Bake for 10 minutes; reduce heat to 300 degrees and bake for 40–50 minutes, or until set.

Spiced Crabapples

9   pounds crabapples
1   pint vinegar
4   pounds sugar
1   teaspoon whole cloves
    Cinnamon sticks, 3 or 4
    Dash of mace

Peel and cut crabapples in half. Place in a large kettle. Add vinegar, sugar, and spices. Boil for a half hour, removing before the apples become too soft.

These can be stored in the refrigerator if they will be used in a short period of time. For long term storage, place in sterilized jars and seal by processing 10-minutes in a boiling water bath.

Two views of the Lincoln home in Springfield, Illinois.

Author's collection.

Photo # b11f19p8 courtesy of Lincoln Home National Historic Site, Springfield, Illinois.

(Upper) the Lincoln dining room in Springfield as it appeared in 1947, and today (lower) after extensive renovation to obtain the look of the home in 1860.

In August 1841, Lincoln traveled to Louisville, Kentucky, to visit his friend Joshua Speed at his family's home, Farmington. Miss Mary Speed, Joshua's older sister, was forty-one years old at the time of Lincoln's visit.

After returning to Springfield, Lincoln wrote to her, saying, "I am literally subsisting on savory remembrances—that is, being unable to eat, I am living upon the remembrance of the delicious dishes of peaches and cream we used to have at your house."

Miss Mary Speed's Peach Pie

Pastry for double crust
   9-inch pie
2   cups peeled, sliced
     peaches
⅓   cup sugar
1   teaspoon lemon juice
2   teaspoon butter
⅓   cups sugar

Preheat oven to 425 degrees. Line a 9-inch pie pan with half of pastry and sprinkle it lightly with ⅓ cup of sugar.

Place peaches in pastry. Pour lemon juice evenly over the peaches. Dot with butter. Sprinkle rest of sugar over the top of the peaches. Cover with remaining pastry. Crimp edges and cut vents in the top of the pastry to permit steam to escape. Brush the pastry top with cream or melted butter. Bake for 10 minutes. Reduce oven temperature to 350 degrees and bake for 35–40 minutes.

Serve warm with whipped cream or vanilla ice cream.

Throughout the years, several newspapers have published this recipe, along with the story by Mrs. Nancy Breedlove that Abraham Lincoln enjoyed this lemon pie while staying at a small hotel when he traveled the Eighth Judicial Circuit of Illinois. §

Meringue-Topped Tart Lemon Custard Pie

CRUST:

1 cup sifted all-purpose flour
¾ teaspoon salt
¼ cup lard
3 to 4 tablespoons cold water

TART LEMON CUSTARD FILLING:

1 cup sugar
1 tablespoon cornstarch

Pinch of salt
Finely grated rind of one large lemon
Juice from one large lemon
⅔ cup water
4 egg yolks
1 egg
2 tablespoons melted butter

MERINGUE:

4 egg whites
3 tablespoons sugar

FOR THE CRUST: Place flour and salt in a large, shallow mixing bowl, and stir well to mix. Add lard and cut in with a pastry blender or knives until texture is that of uncooked oatmeal. Add water, a few drops at a time, mixing briskly with a fork until dough holds together. Turn out on a lightly floured board and roll into a thick circle about 11 inches in diameter. Fit pastry into an 8-inch pie pan, roll overhang under even with rim and crimp.

FOR THE FILLING: Mix sugar, cornstarch, and salt; stir in lemon rind, lemon juice, and water. Add egg yolks, one at a time, beating well after each addition.

§ Temple, *The Taste* **Is** *in My Mouth A Little…Lincoln's Victuals and Potables*, pp. 112–113.

Add the whole egg and beat well. Blend in melted butter. Pour mixture into unbaked pie shell and bake in a preheated oven at 325 degrees for 30 to 35 minutes, until bubbly and begins to thicken. Remove from oven and let stand for 10 minutes. Raise oven temperature to 450 degrees.

FOR THE MERINGUE: Beat egg whites until frothy; continue beating, adding sugar gradually, until meringue peaks softly. Spread gently over lemon filling, making sure meringue touches crimped edges of crust all around. Return to oven and bake 2–3 minutes until meringue is tipped with brown. Cool to room temperature before cutting.

Lemon Custard Pie

⅔ cup water
1 cup sugar
4 eggs, separated
1 lemon
1 tablespoon corn starch
3 tablespoons of sugar
   Unbaked 9-inch pie shell

Preheat oven to 325 degrees. Juice the lemon and grate the rind. Combine water, 1 cup sugar, egg yolks, lemon juice and rind, and corn starch. Beat hard for one minute. Pour mixture into pie shell and bake for 30 minutes.

Beat the egg whites, gradually adding the 3 tablespoons of sugar, until very stiff. Place on custard pie. Increase oven heat to 450 degrees; return pie to oven and bake until meringue peaks brown lightly.

Mary Todd's Courting Cake
(or Burnt Sugar Cake)

1 ½	cups sugar	1 ½	cups cake flour
½	cup hot water	2	teaspoons baking powder
3	egg whites		Dash of salt
½	cup butter	1	teaspoon vanilla

Preheat oven to 350 degrees. Grease and flour two 8-inch cake pans.

Place ½ cup of sugar in a heavy iron skillet. Heat slowly, stirring continuously with a wooden spoon until the sugar becomes a very dark brown. Add hot water and stir until the sugar dissolves and mixture caramelizes.

Beat egg whites, adding ½ cup of sugar a little at a time, until stiff peaks form. Set aside.

In another bowl, cream butter with remaining ½ cup sugar. Sift together cake flour, baking powder, and salt. Alternately add the flour mixture and the caramelized sugar syrup to the butter-sugar mixture. Fold in the beaten egg whites. Add vanilla. Bake for 45 minutes or until done. Finish cake with frosting (recipe follows).

Frosting for Courting Cake

½	cup butter
1	cup dark brown sugar
⅓	cup milk
2	cups powdered sugar

Melt the butter in a heavy saucepan. Add the dark brown sugar and cook over low heat for 2–3 minutes. Stir constantly. Remove from heat. Add milk, and bring to a boil. Cool to lukewarm and gradually stir in powdered sugar. Beat vigorously until mixture is smooth.

Southern Lemon Cake

CAKE:
¾   cup butter
1 ½ cups sugar
4   eggs, separated
1   teaspoon lemon extract
1 ½ cups flour
1 ½ teaspoons baking powder
1   teaspoon salt
¾   cup milk

FILLING:
1   cup sugar
3   tablespoons corn starch
1   cup boiling water
2   eggs
    Juice of 2 large lemons
2   tablespoons butter

FOR CAKE: Grease and flour two 9-inch cake pans. Preheat oven to 350 degrees.

Cream together butter and sugar. Beat egg yolks and add to mixture. Add lemon extract.

Sift together dry ingredients. Alternately add dry ingredients and milk to cream mixture. Beat egg whites until stiff. Fold into batter. Pour into prepared cake pans and bake for 25 minutes. Remove from cake pans and let cool.

FOR FILLING: Mix sugar and corn starch together. Gradually add boiling water. Beat eggs well and add to sugar mixture. Add lemon juice and butter. Cook, stirring constantly until it thickens, about five minutes. Spread on one cooled cake layer and top with remaining cake layer.

If desired, spread Butter Frosting (recipe follows) on the top and the sides of the cake.

Butter Frosting

1	egg white
1	cup granulated sugar
1	cup warm milk
½	cup shortening
½	cup butter
1	teaspoon vanilla

Beat egg white until very stiff. Add sugar slowly. Add milk slowly. Put aside. Beat remaining ingredients well. Add egg mixture a little at a time, beating well after each addition. It will resemble thick whipped cream when done.

Basic Pound Cake

4	sticks butter
2 ½	cups sugar
5	extra large eggs, separated
3	cups flour (measure, then sift it)
1	teaspoon lemon extract
½	teaspoon nutmeg
1	teaspoon mace

Thoroughly cream butter, and add sugar gradually. Add yolks and flour to butter mixture.

Beat egg whites until stiff. Fold spices, extract, and egg whites into flour mixture; fold until well blended. Pour into a fancy tube pan that has greased and dusted with flour. Do not overfill cake pan. Place in an oven that has been preheated to 350 degrees and bake for 75 minutes or until cake tests done in the center. Do not open the oven door prior to this as this may cause the cake to fall. Cool slightly, remove from pan and dust with powdered sugar.

Excellent served with fresh fruit and whipped cream.

Election Cake

(Historic Version)

Make a sponge (as it is called) in the following manner:

Sift into a pan two pounds and a half of flour; and into another plate another pound of flour. Take a second pan, and stir a large tablespoon of the best West India molasses into five gills or two tumblers and a half of strong fresh yeast; adding a gill of water, warm, but not hot.

Then stir gradually into the yeast, &c. the pound of flour that you have sifted separately. Cover it, and let it set by the fire three hours to rise.

While it is rising, prepare the other ingredients by stirring in a deep pan two pounds of fresh butter and two pounds of powdered sugar, till they are light and creamy; adding to them a tablespoon of cinnamon; a teaspoonful of mace; and two powdered nutmegs. Stir in also half a pint of rich milk.

Beat fourteen eggs till very smooth and thick, and stir them gradually into the mixture, alternately with the two pounds and a half of flour which you sifted first.

When the sponge is quite light, mix the whole together, and bake it in buttered tin pans in a moderate oven.

It should be eaten fresh as no sweet cake made with yeast is so good after the first day. If it is not probable that the whole will come to use on the day it is baked, mix but half the above quantity.

Election Cake

1	cup currants
½	cup brandy
1	tablespoon sugar
¾	cup scalded milk
1	cake yeast
¼	cup warm water
1	cup unsifted flour
½	cup butter
1	cup sugar
2 ¼	cups sifted flour
½	teaspoon salt
¾	teaspoon mace
1	teaspoon cinnamon
1	egg
1	teaspoon grated lemon rind
2	teaspoons lemon juice

Soak currants overnight in brandy, in a tightly closed container.

Add the 1 tablespoon sugar to the scalded milk; let cool. Crumble yeast into warm water and let dissolve; add to milk. Add the unsifted flour and mix until well blended. Let rise in a warm place until it has doubled in bulk, about 1 hour.

Cream butter and sugar until very light. Add egg and beat until light. Stir in lemon rind and lemon juice. Add yeast mixture and beat thoroughly. Drain the currants and add to the batter (reserve the brandy). Sifted flour, salt, mace, and cinnamon together. Add dry ingredients and reserved brandy and mix well. Pour into a well-greased tube pan or a 9 by 5-inch loaf pan.

Cover with a cloth and place in a warm place away from a draft. Allow to rise until double in bulk. (This rises very slowly and may take 4 to 6 hours to double in bulk.)

Bake in preheated 375 degree oven for about 45 minutes. Cool in pan briefly. Turn out on a rack and cool further. Brush with Lemon or Orange Glaze.

Lemon or Orange Glaze

1	cup confectioners' sugar
¼	cup lemon or orange juice

Combine sugar and juice. Blend well. Spread thinly over top of cake, allowing the glaze to drizzle down the sides.

Oral history proclaims that when Lincoln was served a fluffy white cake he said that is was the best cake he ever ate. The legend continues that this was the same recipe created by Monsieur Giron, a famous French caterer in Lexington, Kentucky, who had a bakery and dancing hall. The Todd family supposedly was given the recipe for this special cake by Monsieur Giron and treasured it from then on. Members of the family baked it on special occasions, including that evening when Mary Todd wished to impress her beau, Abraham Lincoln, with a special dessert. However, the question is: Is this legend true and was this truly Lincoln's favorite cake?

Emily Helm, Mary's half-sister, had a recipe card labeled "Mary's White Cake" that is believed to be the same white cake recipe from Monsieur Giron's bakery—although the card does not say so. It does not even indicate which "Mary" had the recipe. Considering the close relationship between Emily and Robert Lincoln, there is the small possibility that the recipe belonged to Robert's wife, Mary Harlan Lincoln. No other notation is on the card, nor does any type of icing recipe accompany the cake recipe. It seems that many years ago, someone knew the story about the fancy white cake and assumed this was the correct recipe. Later someone, somehow, added the candied icing recipe. Older cookbooks call for the cake to be baked in a "fluted copper pan,"§ yet other versions call for the batter to be placed in either three round pans or in a rectangular sheet-cake pan. Various versions include different icing recipes, slightly different ingredients, and different methods of preparing the almonds for the batter, but the biggest difference in the recipes is whether or not almonds are listed as an ingredient.

The white cake's story began with Monsieur Mathurin Giron,

---

§ Flexner, *Out of Kentucky Kitchens*, p. 237.

who emigrated from France to Lexington, Kentucky, sometime between the late eighteenth and early nineteenth centuries. He claimed to have been a French grenadier, and in Napoleon's Guard, although most have doubted this was possible because of his height.[†] He was described as an "attractive little figure, rotund and rosy, suave and sunny, scarcely over five feet in height."[††] He preferred French fashions, and, as an exceedingly tactful gentleman, kept his face smooth-shaven. He spoke broken English, and Mary Ann Todd loved to converse with him in his native French language.

Giron's confectionery stood out as one of the most colorful places in Lexington. The charming establishment on Mill Street was a two-story brick building with Tuscan pilasters that supported a balcony of iron lace along the front of the upper story. The confectionary occupied the first floor; the second floor held a ballroom where dancing lessons were given to the city's aristocracy.[†††] In the kitchens of the bakery, Monsieur Giron and his Swiss cook, Dominique Ritter, produced fancy desserts, fruitcakes, tall pyramids of meringues, and candies that delighted the eyes and taste buds of the young Todd children. Elizabeth Humphries Norris, a stepcousin and friend to Mary, wrote, "When Aunt was arranging for a dining or a party we always begged to be allowed to take the written order to Monsieur that we might feast our eyes on the iced cakes decorated with garlands of pink sugar roses, or the bride's cakes with their fountains of clear, spun sugar pyramiding in the center, veiling tiny fat cupids or little sugar brides."[††††]

It is possible that the Todd children were able to partake of those

---

† Doty, *The Confectionery of Monsieur Giron*, p. 4.

†† Ibid. p. 3.

††† Townsend, *Lincoln and the Bluegrass*, p. 64.

†††† Helm, *Mary Wife of Lincoln*, p. 44.

sugar roses and cupids when Elizabeth Todd married Ninian Edwards. Tradition indicates that her wedding cake was created by Monsieur. Although it is not known for certain if he did bake that cake, there is no doubt that he created one honoring the Marquis de Lafayette who, in the spring and summer of 1825, visited several American cities. The American people remembered Lafayette's participation in the American Revolutionary War, and in every city he visited he was honored with parades and community-wide celebrations. He arrived in Lexington in May, and only the kitchen of Monsieur Giron could create a cake spectacular enough to present to the dignitary as a gift from the city's citizens. A mammoth "casellated" cake was created. The Stars and Stripes etched in red, white, and blue tinted icing gloriously adorned the cake. A large cake for a large assembly of people, the original recipe called for six cups of flour and the whites of twenty-four eggs. This recipe set the standard for snow-white cakes, and in honor of the distinguished visitor, it was deemed the Lafayette Cake.

Caroline King, a writer for *The Ladies' Home Journal* during the early part of the twentieth century, claimed that the recipe on the following page was Monsieur Giron's. While it is possible it is his, the inclusion of baking soda indicates that he, or someone else, modified the recipe in the 1840s.[§§]

[§§] King, "Famous Dishes from the Old Kentucky Home," *The Ladies' Home Journal*, p. 143.

Lafayette Cake

(Historic version)

2 cups unsalted butter
4 cups sugar (granulated or powdered)
6 cups flour
1 teaspoon baking soda
2 teaspoons cream of tartar
24 egg whites
Scant teaspoon vanilla extract
½ teaspoon almond extract

Beat butter to a cream, adding gradually four cupfuls of sugar; whip to a white fluff.

Sift six cupfuls of flour with one teaspoonful of soda and two of cream of tartar, three times. Beat to a fine, firm froth the whites of twenty-four eggs.

Add the flour and egg whites alternately to the butter and sugar. Add extracts. Bake the cake, if in a large loaf, in a slow oven for seventy-five to ninety minutes.

Half this recipe will make a fair-sized birthday cake, and one-quarter will provide a cake that will serve from six to eight persons amply.

The Todds used a family sized version of this recipe when in need of a special white cake. It is believed that Mary baked this cake in her Springfield home, and that it was also prepared in the White House kitchen. The recipe carries many names: Mary Todd's White Cake, Mary Todd's Vanilla Almond Cake, Mary's Christmas Cake, and Mary Todd Lincoln's White Almond Cake. But no matter what the recipe is titled, many people believe that Lincoln considered this the best cake that he ever ate.

Mary Todd's Vanilla Almond Cake

1 cup chopped blanched almonds
1 cup butter
6 egg whites
2 cups sugar
3 cups sifted flour
1 teaspoon vanilla or almond extract
1 cup milk
3 teaspoons baking powder
¼ teaspoon salt

Preheat oven to 350 degrees. Grease and flour a bundt or tube cake pan or two 9-inch cake pans. (An old-fashioned fluted copper pan with a center funnel was probably used by Mary Lincoln.)

Grate almonds until they are almost a fine, floury texture. Set aside. Cream butter and sugar; sift flour and baking powder together three times. Add to butter and sugar, alternating with milk. Stir in almonds and beat well.

Beat egg whites with salt until stiff and fold into the cake batter; add vanilla or almond extract. Pour batter into prepared cake pan. Bake for 1 hour or until cake tests done. Turn out on a wire rack and cool.

Frosting
for Mary Todd's Vanilla Almond Cake

The cake may be frosted with either the old-fashioned boiled icing below or a cream cheese icing.

2   cups sugar

1   cup water

2   egg whites, stiffly beaten with a few grains of salt

½   cup diced candied pineapple

½   cup crystallized cherries, cut in half

1   teaspoon vanilla

Boil the sugar and water until the syrup spins a five-inch thread. Slowly fold 4 tablespoons of syrup into the well-beaten egg whites a tablespoon at a time, then add the remaining syrup by slowly pouring it in a thin stream. Beat hard until all is used and the mixture stands in peaks when dropped from a spoon. Add vanilla. Fold in pineapple and cherries.

(Note: If this mixture is not boiled long enough, it will resemble marshmallow cream rather than icing.)

VARIATIONS: Omit the candied fruit from the icing, then cover frosted cake with grated coconut; this is often referred to as a "Merry Christmas Cake." You may also: simply sprinkle powdered sugar over the cake; drizzle cake with a light glaze, such as a lemon-flavored one; or serve warm and plain, accompanied with fresh fruit and ice cream.

To add to the myth of this famed recipe, another slightly different version appears. In 1858, Abraham Lincoln and Stephen A. Douglas were senatorial candidates. During the course of their campaign, the two men met in various cities throughout the state for a series of political debates. According to oral tradition, this version of the white cake was served after the debate in Freeport, Illinois to both men who were guests the home of Jacob J. Oyler and was baked by his daughter, Miss Caroline Oyler. While the story has not been proven as truth, it has added to the legend of white cakes. This version is named in honor of the two candidates.[§]

Lincoln/Douglas Debate Cake

1 ½   cups butter
4   cups fine granulated sugar
5   cups pastry flour
1   teaspoon soda
3   teaspoons cream of tartar
1 ¼   cups milk
1 ½   teaspoons almond extract
16   egg whites, stiffly beaten

Sift together flour, soda, and cream of tartar. Set aside.

Cream butter; then add sugar. Beat for 10 minutes by hand.

Alternately add the flour mixture with the milk, beating constantly. Add almond extract. Fold in beaten egg whites.

Turn into a large tube pan, at least 12 by 4 inches. Bake about 75 minutes in a moderate oven, or until cake tests done.

NOTE: This does make a large amount of batter. The modern baker may wish to cut it in half and bake in a bundt cake pan.

---

§ From www.FoodDownUnder.com

*I*n addition to enjoying the White Cake, Lincoln was also known to have enjoyed the Pecan Cake at the Todd home and declared it his "favorite" cake.

Robert Smith Todd's family was known for lavish entertaining, and their slave butler, Nelson, was well known for his delectable mint juleps. Todd's guests included family and friends who were attorneys, judges, professors, doctors, and statesmen. Dinner was served in the opulent dining room; dessert, brandy, and cigars were served to the men in the back parlor. This was the home Abraham Lincoln and his young family visited in 1847 while en route to Washington after his election as Congressman from Illinois. The visit gave Mary an opportunity to introduce her husband and two young boys (Bobby and Eddie) to her family, and allowed the Todds to display their elegant lifestyle to Lincoln.

During this visit, Lincoln met Henry Clay, the great statesman and friend to Robert Smith Todd. For the second time, Lincoln was introduced to a family whose home was maintained by slave labor (although some of the servants were emancipated). In later years, some of his in-laws would oppose his government.

From the Todd library, Lincoln read *Niles Register* and countless lines of poetry. He committed to memory "Thanatopsis." In the dining room, he enjoyed ambrosial foods prepared by the loving hands of the family cook, Aunt Chaney, and first ate the cake that, according to some, he proclaimed, "best cake I ever ate."[†] Whether Lincoln truly made the comment is unimportant. Most likely, he said several different cakes were his favorite, or the best he ever ate. He enjoyed a good piece of cake, and as a gracious guest, would have told any hostesses that their cake was "the best."

[†] King, "Famous Dishes from the Old Kentucky Home," *The Ladies' Home Journal*, pp. 143–144.

The Todd Pecan cake is rich in flavor and full of nuts and raisins. Although there are many variations of the recipe today, the original is said to have originated in the Todd home. The recipe has been modified somewhat as it includes baking powder, something unknown to the Todd kitchen when Mary was a young girl.

Mary Todd's Pecan Cake

1	cup butter
2	cups granulated sugar
4	cups flour
1	teaspoon baking powder
1	teaspoon baking soda
6	eggs, separated
1	cup orange juice
¾	pound pecan kernels, cut but not chopped
½	grated nutmeg
1	pound raisins, cut into small pieces

Preheat oven to a moderate heat, about 350 degrees.

Sift together flour, baking powder, and baking soda; set aside. Dredge nuts and raisins in ¼ cup of the flour mixture; set aside.

Cream butter well; gradually add sugar. Beat egg yolks until frothy, then add to sugar mixture. Alternately add orange juice and flour mixture. Beat well.

Add pecans and raisins to batter; add nutmeg. Beat egg whites until stiff. Gently fold into batter.

Pour into a well greased and floured pan (tube, fluted, or fancy bundt cake) or into round cake pans. Bake 3–4 hours, depending on the size and shape of the pan. (NOTE: Since early recipes do not always translate easily to accommodate modern ovens and cookware, the cake should be checked frequently. Also, this makes a rather large quantity of batter. Cutting the batter in half will shorten the baking time.)

Caramel Sauce

Mary Todd's Pecan Cake is excellent served with warmed caramel sauce. The secret to making good caramel sauce is timing, so have everything ready before you begin the process.

1   cup sugar
6   tablespoons butter
½   cup heavy whipping cream

Heat sugar on moderately high heat in a heavy bottomed 2- or 3-quart saucepan. (It must be a heavy bottomed pan.) As the sugar begins to melt, stir slowly with a whisk or spoon. When the sugar has melted, it will be amber in color. Immediately add the butter and whisk until melted.

Remove from heat. Count to three, then add the cream and continue to whisk. The mixture will foam up when the cream is added. Whisk until it is smooth and all ingredients are well blended.

Let the sauce cool; pour into a glass jar. Allow to cool to room temperature. This may be stored in the refrigerator for up to two weeks.

On warm summer evenings, young men and women gathered in the upstairs ballroom of Monsieur Giron's establishment for an evening of dancing. When the dancers stepped off the dance floor and looked for a way to quench their thirst, most often they reached for a cup of punch. This Strawberry Punch was a delightful favorite at Monsieur Giron's confectionary and at aristocratic weddings and parties.[§]

Monsieur Giron's Fruit Punch

(Historic recipe)

3	cups sugar
2	cups water
2	cups strawberry juice
1	cup pineapple juice
½	cup orange juice
½	cup lemon juice
1	quart cold water
1	quart orange water ice

Boil together to a thick syrup three cupfuls of sugar and two cupfuls of water.

Cool partially and add strawberry juice, pineapple juice, and lemon juice with a quart of cold water.

Chill for several hours. Pour mixture in a punch bowl containing a quart of orange water ice.

(Orange water ice is made by putting a small amount of orange flavoring, or orange juice, into a quart of water and freezing in to ice. Crush the ice before placing it into the punch bowl.)

---

§ King, "Famous Dishes from the Old Kentucky Home," *The Ladies' Home Journal*, p. 143.

Lincoln's Fruit Cookies

1 ½ cups sugar
1 cup soft butter
1 slightly beaten egg
1 teaspoon grated nutmeg
3 tablespoons dried
    currants or raisins
1 teaspoon baking powder
3 ½ cups flour, approximately
3 tablespoons milk
    (approximately)

Preheat oven to 375 degrees. Cream together butter and sugar. Add slightly beaten egg. Add baking powder and nutmeg. Slowly add just enough flour to make the dough rollable. Add dried fruit. Roll the dough smooth. Cut with a large round cookie cutter and place on well-greased cookie sheet. Moisten the top of each cookie with a little milk. Sprinkle with sugar. Bake for 8–10 minutes. (Be careful not to overbake.) Cool on wire rack or on brown paper.

Sangamon County Sour Cream Cookies

2 eggs
2 cups sifted flour
1 cup sugar
½ teaspoon baking soda
¾ cup sour cream

Beat eggs well. Add sugar and sour cream. Mix together thoroughly. Add sifted flour and baking soda. Beat together. Drop by spoonfuls 1 inch apart on a greased cookie sheet. Bake at 350 degrees for 7–10 minutes, or until a light golden brown. Do not overbake.

Variation: Add ¼ teaspoon cinnamon or cloves to the cookie dough.

The Lincoln family was fond of ice cream and enjoyed it on several occasions. Since ice cream did not last long, people would often hold parties, socials, or family gatherings to share their frozen concoctions. John Todd Stuart wrote of such a gathering at the home of C. M. Smith and his wife Ann, who was Mary Lincoln's sister:

> *"I was invited to come to Cousin Ann's today after church to eat strawberries and ice cream. We had a fine dinner and plenty of cream and berries. Lincoln and Cousin Mary, mother and myself, and Dr. Wallace were there."* †

An oral-tradition story claims that the Lincoln family was fond of Lemon Ice Cream. This recipe appears as it does in a cookbook similar to one belonging to the Lincoln family, and describes the elaborate measures Victorian aristocracy took when preparing food for guests.

Lemon Ice Cream

Have ready two quarts of very rich thick cream and take out one pint. Stir gradually into the pint a pound of the best loaf-sugar powdered fine; and the grated rind and the juice of four ripe lemons of the largest size, or of five or six smaller ones.

If you cannot procure the fruit, you may flavor the cream with essence, or oil of lemon; a teaspoonful or more according to its strength. The strongest and best essence of lemon is white or whitish; when tinged with green, it is comparatively weak having been diluted with water; if quite green, a large teaspoonful will not communicate as much flavor as five or six drops of the white.

---

† John Todd Stuart to his daughter Elizabeth Stuart, Sunday, June 2, 1856. Stuart/Hay Family Papers.

After you have mixed the pint of cream with the sugar and lemon, beat it gradually and hard into the remaining cream—that is the three pints. Cover it, and let it stand to infuse from half an hour to an hour. Then take it, and if you think it necessary, stir in a little more lemon juice or a little more sugar. Strain it into the freezer through a fine strainer (a tin one with small close holes is best) to get rid of the grated lemon peel, which if left in would prevent the cream from being smooth. Cover the freezer and stand it in the ice cream tub, which should be filled with a mixture, in equal quantities, of coarse salt, and ice broken up as small as possible, that it may lie close and compact round the freezer, and thus add to its coldness. Snow, when it can be procured, is still better than ice to mix with the salt. It should be packed closely into the tub, and pressed down hard. Keep turning the freezer about by the handle till the cream is frozen, which it will generally be in two hours.

Occasionally open the lid and scrape down the cream from the sides with a long-handled tin spoon. Take care that no salt goes in, or the cream will be spoiled.

When it is entirely frozen, take it out of the freezer and put it into your mould; set it again in the tub, (which must be filled with fresh ice and salt) and leave it undisturbed till you want it for immediate use. This second freezing, however, should not continue longer than two hours or the cream will become inconveniently and unpleasantly hard, and have much of the flavor frozen out of it. Place the mould in the ice tub, with the head downwards, and cover the tub with pieces of old carpet while the second freezing is going on. When it has arrived at the proper consistence, and it is time to serve it up, dip a cloth in hot water, and wrap it round the mould for a few moments, to loosen the cream and make it come out easily; setting the mould on a glass or chrome dish. If a pyramid or obelisk mould, lift it carefully off the top. If the mould represents doves, dolphins, lap-dogs, fruit baskets; & c., it will open down the middle, and must be taken off in that manner.

Serve it up immediately lest it begin to melt. Serve round sponge cake with it, and wine or cordials immediately after.

If you have no moulds, but intend serving it up in a large bowl or in glasses, it must still be frozen twice over, otherwise it can have no smoothness, delicacy, or consistence, but will be rough and course, and feel in the mouth like broken icicles. The second freezing (if you have no mould) must be done in the freeze, which should be washed out, and set again in the tub with fresh ice and salt. Cover it closely, and let the cream stand in it untouched, but not less than two hours. When you put it into glasses, heap it high on top.

Begin to make ice cream about five or six hours before it is wanted for use. If you commence it too early, it may probably be injured by having to remain too long in the second freezer, as it must not be turned out till a few moments before it is served up. In damp weather it requires a longer time to freeze.

If cream is scarce, mix with it an equal quantity of rich milk, and then add, for each quart, two tablespoons of powdered arrow-root rubbed in a little cold milk.

Orange ice cream is made in the same manner as lemon.

Velvety Lemon Ice Cream

(quick modern version)

2 ½ cups cold, heavy
      whipping cream
2 ½ cups cold half-and-half
2   cups sugar
1   cup fresh lemon juice
    Zest from 1 large lemon
1   to 1 ½ teaspoons lemon
      extract

Add all ingredients together in a chilled bowl. Stir until sugar is dissolved. Refrigerate until mixture is well chilled, at least 4 hours.

Pour mixture into ice cream maker and process according to directions.

NOTE: This recipe works well for electric ice cream makers, such as Cuisinart, or stand mixers that have a freezer bowl attachment, such as for Kitchen Aid.)

Strawberry Parties

When John Todd Stuart wrote to his daughter about dining at the home of Ann Smith, he mentioned the ice cream for dessert and the plentiful amount of strawberries. The Todds were enjoying what many Victorians enjoyed—an almost love affair with berries.

The nineteenth century saw strawberries elevated from a springtime treat found in some woodlands to an elaborate delicacy worthy of parties and festivals devoted to its sweet pulp.

How did this transformation of the strawberry begin? Like so many trends, it most likely began in literature. In 1815, Jane Austen published her novel, *Emma*, which told of a garden party where the guests ate strawberries which were described as "hautboy infinitely superior—no comparison the others hardly eatable."[†] Europe's aristocracy became fascinated with the strawberry. Growers developed a musk strawberry with mottled red or red-violet skin whose fragrant hallmark was a "floral, spicy, aroma—the taste of honey, musk, and wine."[††] And wealthy Europeans wanted more. During the journey of Queen Isabella II of Spain from Atocha Station to Real Sitio, the train's dining car served tarts with wild strawberries. When the public learned of this delicacy, they wanted the same treat served in their own homes. In fact, strawberries became so popular throughout Europe that "strawberry trains" were soon carrying the fruit from the growers to markets in major cities.

As strawberry fever swept over the Continent, it was not long before it moved across the Atlantic and Americans began clamoring

---

[†] Karp, David, "Berried Treasure," July 2006, www.smithsonianmag.com
[††] Ibid.

for the red fruit. In 1843, strawberry growers in Cincinnati, Ohio, were the first to ship their produce using refrigerated rail cars. Ice was packed on top of boxes of strawberries to keep them fresh as they traveled to other parts of the country. Just as an "oyster line" had been established to transport oysters to the Midwest, "strawberry lines" helped bring fresher fruit to the prairies. Soon Americans across the country were enjoying strawberry parties in their homes, at church socials, and at community functions.§

Ann Smith was not the only member of the Todd clan to entertain during the strawberry season. Mary Lincoln held several strawberry parties in Springfield and in Washington. In Springfield and other parts of the United States the "berry season" continued beyond the growing season of strawberries and continued into the summer months when raspberries and blackberries were at their ripest. Mary enjoyed all of the berry parties. On June 26, 1859, Mary wrote to her friend Hannah Shearer:

> "For the last two weeks, we have had a continual round of strawberries parties, this last week I have spent five evenings out—and you may suppose, that this day of rest, I am happy to enjoy. . . . This last week, we gave a strawberry company of about seventy, and I need not assure you, that your absence was sadly remembered. . . . After raspberry time, we will resume, doubtless our usual quiet."§§

In Washington Mary continued berry parties. In 1861, she had a black silk day dress made that was most likely worn at such events. The fabric is embroidered with large bunches of purple and white

---

§ Ibid.
§§ Turner, p. 56.

This black silk day dress, made in 1861, was festooned with elaborate silk-embroidered bunches of purple and white leaves and berries elegantly spaced on the gown. Between the bunches are small clusters of green leaves and red berries that appear to be either strawberries or raspberries, either of which would have been appropriate in light of Mary's penchant for berry parties, a custom she carried from Springfield to the White House.
(Courtesy of Collection of the Lincoln Financial Foundation, Ft. Wayne, IN; #4523 [identified as ML, O-8].)

leaves. Between the large bunches are small clusters of green leaves and red berries. One can imagine Mary wearing this gown while her guests enjoyed strawberries and cream.

On one occasion a vast amount of strawberries proved to be too much temptation for young Tad. The gardener, Mr. Watt had been forcing the berries in the conservatory with the intent of having them served at a state dinner. Tad spied them and ate them all, thus causing Mr. Watt to remark about "the Madam's wildcat."[†††]

Since berries spoil easily, Victorian housewives used those not eaten fresh to make jellies, preserves, and even vinegar. Some berries were dried in the sunshine to be used during the winter for baked breads, cakes, and puddings.

What was served at Mary's strawberry parties is unknown. Bowls of fresh berries would have been served along with cakes and ice cream. In addition to raspberry shrubs, she may have served her guests strawberry punch. (We can assume that strawberries were also used for shrubs and raspberries were made into punch.) Included here are traditional strawberry recipes which may have been served at any of the strawberry parties held or attended by the Lincoln family.

---

††† Randall, p. 277.

Old-fashioned Shortcake

2   cups all-purpose flour
⅓   cup sugar
1   tablespoon baking
     powder
½   teaspoon salt
½   cup shortening
¾   cup milk
2   eggs, beaten

Sift together all dry ingredients. Cut in shortening with a pastry blender until the texture resembles fine crumbs. In a separate bowl, beat together milk and eggs. Pour into dry ingredients all at once and mix with a fork until moistened. (Do not over-mix) Dust your hands with flour, and handling the dough as little as possible, pat the dough into a 9-inch round cake pan. Bake at 375 for 25–30 minutes. Cut into wedges and serve hot with topping of fresh strawberries and ice cream, thick cream, or whipping cream.

Strawberry Cake Frosting

⅓   cup butter
2   tablespoons milk
     Dash of salt
1   teaspoon vanilla extract
1   tablespoon pureed
     strawberries
2 ½ to 3 cups confectioners'
     sugar

In a small saucepan melt butter, stir in milk, salt, and vanilla. Heat until hot but not boiling. Add pureed strawberries and enough confectioners' sugar to make the mixture desired consistency for frosting.

Spicy Strawberry Jam Cake

1 ½ cups flour
1 teaspoon baking powder
½ teaspoon baking soda
¼ teaspoon salt
1 teaspoon cinnamon
1 teaspoon nutmeg
½ teaspoon ground cloves
¾ cup butter, softened
1 cup light brown sugar
2 eggs, well beaten
3 tablespoons sour cream
1 cup strawberry jam
½ cup chopped nuts

Sift together flour, baking powder, soda and salt. Stir in spices. Set aside. In a separate bowl, cream butter and sugar until very light. Beat in eggs and sour cream. Stir flour mixture into liquid mixture and mix only until ingredients are blended. Stir in jam; add nuts. Pour batter into a 7-inch greased tube pan. Bake at 350 degrees for 30 minutes. Remove when cake tests done by inserting toothpick into center.

Strawberry Nut Loaf

3 cups flour, sifted
2 cups sugar
1 teaspoon salt
1 teaspoon baking soda
2 teaspoons cinnamon
¼ teaspoon nutmeg
4 eggs, beaten
1 ¼ cups vegetable oil
2 cups fresh strawberries, sliced
1 cup chopped pecans

Sift together flour, sugar, salt, soda, and spices. In a separate bowl, blend together eggs and oil. Gradually stir into dry ingredients alternately with strawberries. Fold in pecans. Pour batter into two greased and floured loaf pans. Bake at 350 degrees for 45–50 minutes.

Fresh Strawberry Pie

1	quart whole strawberries
1	9-inch prebaked pie shell
⅓	cup honey
½	cup sugar
¼	cup water
3	tablespoons cornstarch
¼	teaspoon butter
1	cup heavy cream, whipped

Select 10 to 12 attractive berries; set aside. Arrange half of remaining berries in pie shell.

Combine honey, sugar, water, cornstarch, and salt in a saucepan. Slice remaining berries into the mixture and cook over medium heat, stirring, until sauce thickens. Remove from heat and stir in butter. Let mixture cool, then pour into the pie shell over the fresh berries. Refrigerate until well chilled. Spread the whipped cream evenly over the pie and decorate the top with the reserved berries.

Strawberry Jam

1	quart fresh strawberries
1	quart sugar
	Juice of half a lemon

Combine strawberries and sugar in a large, heavy-bottomed saucepan. Bring to a slow boil, stirring with a wooden spoon. Try to keep the berries whole. When mixture begins to boil, let it continue to do so for 15 minutes, stirring only occasionally. Remove from heat and let cool. Gently stir in the lemon juice. Skim off any white foam that may appear on top of the mixture. Pour into hot, sterilized jars and seal using a boiling water-bath method, or refrigerate jam until ready for use.

Strawberry Buckle

½	stick butter, softened
¾	cup sugar
1	egg, beaten
½	teaspoon vanilla
½	cup milk
2	cups sifted cake flour
2	teaspoons baking powder
½	teaspoon salt
2	cups fresh strawberries, sliced

TOPPING:

½	stick butter
½	cup brown sugar
⅓	cup flour, sifted
½	teaspoon cinnamon
	Dash of nutmeg

In a large bowl, cream together sugar and butter until light and fluffy. Blend in eggs and vanilla, then milk. In a separate bowl sift together dry ingredients. Stir into liquid mixture. Fold in berries. Spread into a greased floured 9 by 9-inch baking pan.

For the topping, cream butter and sugar together. Blend in flour and cinnamon until mixture is crumbly. Sprinkle topping mixture over batter and sprinkle the nutmeg over top. Bake at 375 degrees for 30–35 minutes. Serve warm with cream.

Strawberry Ice Cream

(Modern version)

1	quart fresh strawberries
1	scant cup sugar
2	cups half-and-half
2	cups heavy cream

Hull berries. Wash and put through a sieve. Add sugar and half-and-half. Whip the heavy cream until it is stiff, then blend into mixture. Pour mixture into ice cream maker and freeze according to directions.

Inaugural Journey

1861

The Astor House in New York City.

Illustration by Amy Castleberry.

On November 6, 1860, the Lincoln family waited, as did the nation, as the election returns came in. Mary waited at home while Mr. Lincoln went to the room reserved for him at the State House. That evening they attend a special supper hosted by the Republican ladies held at Watson's Confectionery. Lincoln's campaign supporters and friends crowded into the capitol to hear the election returns. Later in the evening, Lincoln and a group of friends were in the telegraph office receiving the news of the returns. Lyman Trumbull was one of the first to say, "If we get New York that settles it." The man receiving the telegram became very excited as the message arrived saying that New York had gone Republican.

Lincoln, who had been standing in the doorway when the first shout went up, realized the nation was in crisis and that his responsibilities would be great. Crowd members began shouting, throwing up their hats, and slapping one another on the back. The Rail Splitter had won.

Lincoln turned to his friend Trumbull and said, "I guess I'll go down and tell Mary about it." And with that, he turned and headed towards the home on Eighth and Jackson. Mary, while awaiting the news, had fallen asleep. She was confident her husband would be elected. Somewhere between her dreams and reality she knew her confidence had been rewarded. Lincoln relayed the story of telling Mary the good news to the editor of *The Independent*, Henry C. Bowen:

I told my wife to go to bed, as probably I should not be back before midnight. . . . On my arrival I went to my bedroom and found my wife sound asleep. I gently touched her shoulder and said, "Mary"; she made no answer. I spoke again, a little louder, saying, "Mary, Mary! we are elected!"[†]

[†] Randall, *Mary Lincoln: Biography of a Marriage*, pp. 185–188.

On the morning of February 11, 1861, Abraham Lincoln, his son Robert, and some companions boarded a train to begin the inaugural journey to the nation's capital. Mary, the youngest two boys, and several of Mary's relatives would leave later that day and meet the party in Indianapolis, Indiana. From there, they would continue the journey to Washington together. Along the way, the Lincolns witnessed lines of people waving flags and cheering the President-elect and his family. At every stop, crowds gathered to catch a glimpse of the family. Often, Lincoln appeared at the back of the train and waved to the crowd, but he made few speeches.

Welcoming committees and receptions awaited the Lincolns in several larger cities. In Erie, Pennsylvania, it was reported that Lincoln was offered wine to drink but declined. He remarked that he did not indulge in liquor; however, he apparently indulged in sweets. It was reported that he requested a second piece of mince pie that had been baked by Mrs. Thomas B. Moore.[†]

[†] Searcher, *Lincoln's Journey to Greatness*, p. 114.

Mince Pie

This historic recipe comes from the White House kitchen. Mince meat was prepared in advance and could be stored for several months. This recipe makes enough filling for several large pies. Due to the richness of the mince, this is excellent when used in small tart pastry.

2   pounds lean, fresh beef, cooked, cooled, and cut into fine pieces

1   pound beef suet, cleaned of strings and minced to powder

5   pounds apples, washed, peeled, and sliced

2   pounds raisins

1   pound Sultana raisins

2   pounds currants

¾   pound citron, cut up fine

2   tablespoons cinnamon

1   tablespoon powdered nutmeg

2   tablespoons mace

1   tablespoon ground cloves

1   tablespoon allspice

1   tablespoon fine salt

2 ¼ pounds brown sugar

1   quart brown sherry

1   pint brandy

Mix together well. Place in a jar, cover tightly, and set in a cool place. Or, place in sterilized jar and process with a 10-minute boiling water bath to seal jars.

When baking a 9-inch pie, place a prepared crust in the bottom of the pie pan. Fill with mince filling—this usually takes 3 to 4 cups of filling. If desired, thin apple slices may be placed on top of the filling. Top with second crust. Crimp edges. Vent the center. Bake at 425 degrees for 30–35 minutes.

*I*n Syracuse, the crowd waiting to welcome Lincoln and his party contained ten thousand people. Lunch was brought aboard the train and was prepared under the direction of Dean Richmond. Enjoyed by the Lincolns and their guests, the meal consisted of "various dishes including chicken, turkey, bread, cake, handed around by waiters."[§]

On February 19, the Lincolns arrived at the Astor House where the south room of Suite 37 was reserved for Mary Lincoln. At six P.M., dinner was served in a private dining room to a party of ten. A Broadway florist placed a nosegay of flowers at each place setting. The center of the table held a "mound of white camellias, red roses, and violets set in a bed of yellow pansies and green fern trimmed with tricolored satin ribbon."[§§] An assortment of fresh fruits and flowers were displayed on a side table. And for the first time during the inaugural trip, the press published a reception menu.

---

§ Searcher, p. 149.
§§ Ibid. p. 188.

Menu

FEBRUARY 19, 1861

Reception of

HON. ABRAHAM LINCOLN
President-elect

Soup
Julian (sic)

Fish
Boiled salmon, anchovy sauce

Cold Dishes
Tureen of goose liver
Boned turkey with jelly

Vegetables
Boiled potatoes
Turnips, cream sauce
Baked mashed potatoes
Green peas
Beets   Lettuce   Celery

Relevés
Fillet of beef, larded,
with green peas
Larded sweetbreads, tomato sauce
Fillet of chicken, truffle sauce
Shrewsbury oysters, baked in shell

Game
Roast canvas back duck
Roast stuffed quail

Pastry
Charlotte russe
Champagne jelly
Cream cakes
Cup custards

French cream cakes
Claret jelly
Ladies' fingers
Kisses

Fruits
All kinds in season

Ice Cream

Julienne Soup

Carrots
Turnips
Celery
Water
Salt
Pepper
2 quarts soup stock

Cut carrots and turnips into quarter inch pieces in the shape of dice. Cut celery into thin slices. Cover these with boiling water; add salt and pepper. Cook until vegetables are soft.

In another saucepan bring two quarts of soup stock to a boil. Add cooked vegetables and the water to the stock. Add more seasoning if necessary. Serve hot.

In the spring and summer, asparagus, peas, and string beans can be used. Cut all vegetables into uniform thickness.

Historically, a soup stock was made from cooking bits of meat and bones in water; then running the stock through a sieve or cheese cloth to remove the bits of solid material. Modern cooks can purchase prepared broth in many forms.

Anchovy Sauce

8 anchovies
1 quart water
2 glasses of red wine
2 cups melted butter

Soak the anchovies for three to four hours; change the water every hour. Place in a sauce pan with one quart of cold water. Simmer until the anchovies are entirely dissolved and the liquid is diminished to about two-thirds.

Strain the liquid. Stir in red wine and add to melted butter. Heat mixture again, and serve with salmon or fresh cod.

Larded Sweetbreads

Sweetbreads are the two large glands lying in the back of the throat and the breast, and have a delicate flavor. Veal sweetbreads are considered the best. Because they spoil very quickly, they should be placed in cold water as soon as purchased and parboiled before using them in any form.

2   sweetbreads
1   tablespoon of lemon juice
     Salt
     Water
     Lard or strips of bacon

To LARD: Thread a strip of fat or fatty bacon through holes made in the sweetbread. This will keep them from drying out while cooking them.

To COOK: Place sweetbreads in cold water. Remove the pipes and membranes. Add salt and lemon juice to boiling water. Cook sweetbreads in rolling boiling water for 20 minutes. Plunge into cold water to harden.

To SERVE: Place sweetbreads on a serving platter and cover in tomato sauce.

Tomato Sauce

1   quart canned tomatoes
1   slice onion
2   cloves
     Small amount of pepper
       and salt
1   ounce butter
1   tablespoon flour

Place tomatoes, onion, cloves, salt and pepper in a pan. Cook on a low boil over medium heat for about 20 minutes. Remove from heat and strain mixture. In another pan, melt butter. Sprinkle in flour; stir until it browns and froths a little. Mix in tomato pulp. Sauce is ready to serve.

Truffle Sauce

Truffles are good only when in season and are very fresh.

2	ounces butter
18	truffles
	Brown or white gravy
	Salt
	Juice of half a lemon

Wash and slice truffles. Add butter to truffles and simmer together until the truffles are tender. Add as much gravy as desired to bring it to its proper thickness. (Use either white or brown, depending on the choice of meat) Season as desired with salt. Squeeze the juice of half a lemon into sauce.

Shrewsbury Oysters, Baked in Shell

Shrewsbury oysters came from the East River in New York. They were famous world-wide and were considered a delicacy.

Vice President Hannibal Hamlin related in later years, "When oysters on the half shell were served, Lincoln looked at them quizzically as if he had never partaken of such a dish before. 'Well, I don't know that I can manage these things,' he said solemnly, 'but I guess I can learn.' That put everyone at ease and provided a delightful conversation piece." §

Use large oysters on the half-shell. Put a piece of butter on each oyster; sprinkle with salt and pepper to taste. Place in a hot oven and bake for 2–3 minutes or until the edges curl. The addition of lemon juice or catsup adds flavor.

---

§ Searcher, *Lincoln's Journey to Greatness*, p. 204.

Lady Fingers

Lady fingers are used for lining molds that are filled with whipped cream mixtures and are often served with frozen desserts. They are also frequently served with Charlotte Russe.

3	egg whites	Beat egg whites until stiff and dry.
⅓	cup powdered sugar	Gradually add sugar and continue beating.
2	egg yolks	Beat egg yolks and beat mixture until
⅓	cup flour	thick and lemon colored. Add flavoring.
⅛	teaspoon salt	Cut and fold in the flour mixed with salt.
¼	teaspoon vanilla	

Using a pastry bag and tube, shape cakes 4 ½ inches long and 1 inch wide on a tin sheet that has been covered with unbuttered baking paper.

Sprinkle with powdered sugar and bake for 8 minutes in a moderate oven. Remove from paper with a knife.

Charlotte Russe

(Historic version)

Most nineteenth-century cookbooks include instructions for several different types of Charlottes Russe. Some are flavored with chocolate. Some are considered "basic" and others are identified as being "fine." This historic version from an old White House cookbook is considered "fine." [†]

Whip one quart of rich cream to a stiff froth, and drain well on a nice sieve. To one scant pint milk, add six eggs beaten very light; make very sweet. Flavor high with vanilla.

Cook over hot water till it is a thick custard. Soak one full ounce of Cox's

---

† Gilette and Ziemann, *The White House Cookbook*, p. 320.

gelatin in a very little water, and warm over hot water. When custard is very cold, beat in lightly the gelatin and the whipped cream.

Line the bottom of your mold with buttered paper, the side with sponge cake or lady fingers fastened together with the white of one egg. Fill with the cream, put in a cold place or in summer on ice. To run out, dip the mold for a moment in hot water.

In draining the whipped cream, all that drips through can be rewhipped.

Charlotte Russe

(Modern version)

1	tablespoon unflavored gelatin
¼	cup cold water
½	cup milk
½	cup sugar
1	pint cream
1	cup milk
½	teaspoon vanilla
	Lady fingers or sponge cake

Soak gelatin in cold water. Scald ½ cup milk, and then add sugar, gelatin, and vanilla. Chill until slightly set. Next whip cream. Dilute with 1 cup milk. Fold into gelatin. Line a mold or fancy bowl with lady fingers or sponge cake. Pour in cream mixture. Decorate with maraschino cherries. Keep refrigerated.

Kisses

According to a White House cookbook, kisses were to be served for dessert at large dinners with other suitable confectionary. They were to be made a day in advance and served on a high glass dish. Often, half would be tinted a pale pink and the others were served white.[§]

4	egg whites
1	pound powdered sugar
8	drops of lemon extract (or other flavoring if desired)
	Currant jelly (or other flavor)

Beat the egg whites until they stand alone. Then gradually beat in powdered sugar, one teaspoonful at a time. Add eight drops of extract and beat the mixture very hard.

Lay a wet sheet of paper on the bottom of a square tin pan. Dab just a small amount of the egg white mixture onto the pan, about two inches apart. On each dab of mixture, place a small teaspoonful of stiff jelly. With a large spoon, pile some of the beaten egg mixture on each lump of jelly, so as to cover it entirely. Drop on the mixture as evenly as possible, so as to make the kisses of a round, smooth shape.

Set them in a cool oven, and as soon as they are colored, they are done. Take them out, and place two bottoms of the kisses together. Lay them lightly on a sieve, and dry them in a cool oven till the two bottoms stick fast together so as to form a ball or oval.

[§] Gilette and Ziemann, p. 330.

Wine or Champagne Jelly

(Historic version)

The Lincolns' dinner menu included Champagne and claret jellies. Both could be made by using this historic version recipe.

Pour a pint of cold water over the contents of a package of Cox's gelatin. Let it soak for ten minutes then add a pint of boiling water and stir until gelatin is dissolved. Next add a pint of wine, half a pound of sugar, the grated rind of a lemon and its juice, a little grated nutmeg, ground cloves, and cinnamon.

Stir the beaten whites of two eggs into this mixture and set on a slow fire and stir until it starts to boil, when it should be immediately taken off and strained through a jelly bag. Rinse the bag in boiling water first and suspend it near the fire until strained. Wet a mold with cold water before putting in the jelly, and set on ice to cool.

Wine Jelly

(Modern version)

6	envelopes unflavored gelatin	2	cups sugar
2	cups cold water	1	pint fine dry sherry
6	cups boiling water	3	tablespoons brandy
3	lemons (grated peel and juice)		Whipped cream, sweetened with a bit of sugar
	Pinch of salt		Food coloring

Sprinkle gelatin on cold water. Add sugar, salt, and lemon. Add boiling water and stir well to dissolve thoroughly. When cool, stir in brandy, sherry, and food coloring. Pour into molds that have been rinsed in cold water. Chill until set. Turn out onto serving plate and serve with slightly sweetened whipped cream. Garnish with orange slices and strawberries if desired.

The following day held a busy schedule for the Lincoln family. Lincoln attended a breakfast at the home of Moses Grinnell's daughter. Grinnell was a New York businessman and had invited nearly one hundred of the city's elite businessmen to meet the President-elect. During the afternoon Mary and Willie attended a viewing of Wilkie Collins play *Woman in White* and Barnum's Museum. After dinner that evening, Mary held a reception with Mrs. James Watson Webb, whose husband was the former editor of *Courier & Enterprise*. While the ladies entertained themselves at the reception, several of the gentlemen, including Lincoln, Judge Davis, and Alderman Cornell attended a showing of Verdi's opera *Un ballo in maschera*.[†]

Prior to the evening reception, the presidential party enjoyed dinner. It was seven o'clock, an hour later, before everyone was seated in the dining room for another gastronomic event. The room was decorated much in the same manner as the previous evening and fresh bouquets of flowers graced each of the eleven plates. Joining the Lincolns that evening were Vice-President elect Hannibal Hamlin and his wife, Ellen. Mary's sister Elizabeth Edwards and her husband, Ninian, and their daughter (also named Elizabeth) had arrived from Springfield. They would continue to Washington to assist Mary and attend the social ceremonies at the White House.

This evening, the Astor House printed its menu in French. Besides being the chosen *languor* of the gourmet, French was spoken very well by Mary Lincoln.

---

† The Lincoln Institute, "Mr. Lincoln and New York." www.mrlincolnandnewyork.org.

Carte du Diner

Huîtres en coquilles cru

Potage
Potage Brunoise, aux oeufs pochés

Piéce Froide
Pain de gibier, en Bellevue

Poisson
Alose farcies, braises, sauce au vin de Champagne

Relevés
Duides bouillie, aux Huîtres

Entrées
Cailles, farcies, aux Champignones
Côtelettes d' Agneau, aux petites pommes de terre frites, au Beurre
Timbale de Volaille, à la Toulouse
Arcade de Perdrix, à la financer

Légumes
Pommes de terre, bouillies Pommes de terre, au gratin
Epinards, aux oeufs Petits Pois à la française
Navets, au lait Betteraves
Celeri Laitue

Gibier
Canard de Canvas Back

Patisseries
Gâteaux, à la Française   Charlotte Russe Marigner Suisse

Gelée au vin de Champagne Gelée au vin de Bordeaux

Macarons, aux Amandes   Gâteaux de Lafayette

Fruit
Glacé, à la Vanille

Maison d'Astor, 20 Fevrier, 1861

These sparkling crystal goblets were among the set used by Lincoln's entourage on the train along his trip from Springfield to Washington.

(Both photos this page: LR734, courtesy Abraham Lincoln Presidential Library and Museum, Springfield, Illinois.)

Stuffed Shad, Braised in Champagne Sauce

ALOSE FARCIES, BRAISES, SAUCE AU VIN DE CHAMPAGNE

Because no exact recipe accompanying the dinner card for this meal exists, it is impossible to know exactly what type of stuffing was served with the fish. Following are two possible choices, both of which can be served with Champagne Sauce on page 116.

Majestic Stuffed Shad

1	dressed shad (about 3 pounds)
½	pound shad roe
½	pound crab meat
	Salt and pepper to taste
2	tablespoons butter
1	medium onion, thinly sliced
4	strips bacon

Wash and dry fish thoroughly. Place in a shallow, foil lined baking dish. Open the fish.

Mash roe and spread over the bottom part of the fish cavity. Remove cartilage from the crab meat and spread over roe. Sprinkle with salt and pepper. Dot with butter. Close the fish over the stuffing. Sprinkle the top of the fish with salt and pepper. Place the onion slices and bacon strips on top of the fish. Loosely cover with foil and bake for 45–50 minutes at 350 degrees. Serves 6–8.

Stuffed Shad

1   boneless roe shad
       (1–2 pounds)
¼   cup minced white onions
¼   cup minced bell pepper
¼   cup minced celery
4   tablespoons butter
8   ounces shad roe
½   cup seasoned bread
       crumbs
       Salt and pepper to taste
3   pieces of bacon cut in
       half
       Juice from one medium
       sized lemon

Melt butter. Sauté onion, bell pepper, and celery until tender. Add breadcrumbs. Break up the roe and add to mixture. Add salt and pepper. Mix well, and cook lightly.

Place shad in a buttered dish with the flesh side up. Stuff cavities of shad where the bones have been removed. Place a little bit of water around the edge of the fish to prevent it from drying out during cooking. Cover and bake for 20–25 minutes at 375 degrees. When about three minutes of cooking time is left, place bacon across the top of the fish. Drip the juice of the lemon on top of the fish. Return to oven and finish cooking. Serves 4–6.

Champagne Sauce

½   pound fresh mushrooms
     Salt and pepper
6   tablespoons butter
5   shallots, finely minced
6   egg yolks
1   bottle champagne
1 ¾   cups crème fraîche

Clean and slice mushrooms into julienne strips.

Heat 3 tablespoons butter in a large skillet. Add shallots and sauté gently over low heat. Add remaining 3 tablespoons of butter and mushrooms. Cook until tender; transfer to a bowl and cover.

Using the same skillet, deglaze it with the champagne. Bring the liquid to a rapid boil and cook until reduced by one half. Whisk crème fraiche and egg yolks together until smooth.

Over low heat, gradually spoon the crème fraiche mix into the skillet and cook until slightly thickened. Do not boil mixture once the crème fraiche has been added! Season with salt and pepper.

Place stuffed shad (your choice of one of the previous shad recipes) on a platter and cover with sauce. Place until the broiler for a few seconds. Remove to a serving platter and add mushrooms and shallots. Serve immediately. Serves 6.

NOTE: Crème fraîche is similar to sour cream but it has a higher fat content. It can be made in the following manner: Combine 1 cup double cream and 2 tablespoons buttermilk. Place in a clean glass jar and refrigerate for 6–8 hours before use.

French Peas

Petits pois à la française

½ small head lettuce, washed
1 pound fresh peas
3 spring onion, chopped
2 tablespoons water
2 ounces butter
½ teaspoon salt
¼ teaspoon pepper
1 clove garlic, minced
 Pinch of flour
1 teaspoon castor sugar
1 teaspoon fresh rosemary, or ½ teaspoon dried

Put butter in a sauce pan. Slice lettuce in long shreds. Add half of the lettuce to the butter. Top with remaining ingredients. Add remaining lettuce on top.

Cover and bring to a boil. Lower heat and simmer for 15 minutes. Stir a few times during cooking so not to scorch vegetables.

Lamb Cutlets with Small Potatoes in Butter

Côtelettes d'Agneau, aux petites pommes de terre frites, au Beurre

This version is taken from a nineteenth-century White House cookbook.

Wash and peel some good potatoes and cut them into slices the thickness of a small coin. The quantity of potatoes must be decided according to the number of persons being served; allow two or three potatoes for each person. After the potatoes are sliced, wash them two or three times to cleanse them. Arrange them neatly in layers in a brown stone dish proper for baking purposes. Sprinkle a little salt and pepper between each layer, and add a sufficient quantity of cold water and butter to prevent burning. Place the dish in a very hot oven for a few minutes to brown the potatoes. Have ready some lamb cutlets. Trim off most of the fat. Shape the cutlets into a nice round shape and place a small skewer through each. When the potatoes are nicely browned, remove the dish from the oven, and place the cutlets on top. Add more salt and pepper, and more water if required. Return the dish to a cooler oven and bake for about 45 minutes, until the cutlets are sufficiently cooked. During the cooking process, when the upper sides of the cutlets are a nice crisp brown, turn them over so as to brown the other side. If the potatoes appear to be dry, add a little more hot water. Be sure the water is hot, not cold, as cold water will increase the cooking time.

When cutlets are done, remove from oven and serve hot. Do not turn out onto another dish, as this will spoil the appearance of the potatoes.

Preparation in this manner allows the drippings and gravy from the meat to drip among the potatoes. If a modern cook does not wish for the potatoes to be cooked in meat drippings, it is possible to prepare the cutlets in a moderate oven. Prepare the cutlets in the same manner being sure to place sufficient amounts of water, and salt and pepper to taste. The potatoes can be gently fried in butter on a stove top. When ready to serve, place a cutlet on the plate, and surround it with the fried potatoes.

Spinach with Egg

EPINARDS, AUX OEUFS

Trim off the roots and tough stalks of half a peck of spinach. Wash in cold, salted water being sure to remove all particles of dirt or debris.

Boil water that has a small amount of salt added. Once water is at a rolling boil, add spinach and cook for three minutes or until tender. Do not allow spinach to become soft and watery.

Drain spinach. Place in a large pan of cold water until leaves are cool, and then chop very fine. Place spinach over heat again. Add palatable amounts of butter, salt, and pepper.

While the spinach is being heated, poach six eggs to a soft stage. Place spinach on a serving dish and lay eggs on top of spinach. Serve hot. Serves 6.

Potatoes au Gratin

POMMES DE TERRE, AU GRATIN

Peel and boil about 2 pounds of white potatoes until tender. Season with salt and pepper to taste. Cool. Slice potatoes into thick slices or half-inch cubes.

1	tablespoon butter	Melt butter in a saucepan over low to
1	tablespoon flour	medium heat. Add other ingredients in
½	teaspoon salt	the order given. Slowly add milk being
¼	teaspoon white pepper	careful not to scald the milk. Cook until
1	cup milk	slightly thickened.

Butter a baking dish. Put in a layer of sauce, then a layer of potatoes. Continue until all ingredients are in the dish.

To one cupful of dried and sifted bread crumbs, add 1 teaspoon of melted butter and stir until it is evenly mixed. Spread over the contents of the baking dish and place in a quick oven [about 375 degrees] for 20 minutes, or until nicely browned.

For variations in flavor, add a little onion juice, chopped parsley, or grated cheese to the sauce.

Sugar Beets

BETTERAVES

Wash beets trimming the leaves and roots, but not breaking the skin.

Place in a large pot that is half full of boiling water. Boil beets until tender. If beets are small, this will take about 45 minutes. Medium beets will take about an hour, but all beets, even those that are quite large, should cook within two hours.

When beets are done, rub off the skins with a wet towel. Slice them and dress them with salt, pepper, and butter to taste. Serve at once.

White Turnips in Cream Sauce

NAVETS AU LAIT

Slice or cut into small pieces 5 or 6 turnips. Cook in boiling water until tender. Keep warm while preparing sauce.

2	tablespoons butter
1 ½	tablespoons flour
1	cup scalded cream
¼	teaspoon salt
	Few grains pepper

Put butter in sauce pan, stir until melted and bubbling; add flour mixed with salt and pepper, and stir until thoroughly blended.

Pour in scalded cream gradually adding about ⅓ cup at a time. Stir until well mixed, and then beat until smooth and glossy.

Place cooked turnips in a casserole or baking dish. Pour cream sauce over turnips. Serve hot.

The Astor House listed a "game" course on the dinner cards representing the dinners served to President Lincoln and his guests. Game birds were a staple in the Lincoln household during his youth. This basic method of roasting fowl was used in the kitchens of famous restaurants and over the hearths in frontier log cabins.

Canvas Back Duck

CANARD DE CANVAS BACK

After cleaning the duck, wipe it completely dry. Rub skin with fat or butter inside and out. Rub with salt and pepper.

Stuff the duck cavity in the same manner as any other fowl.

Roast about an hour and make a gravy out of the giblets and wings. Boil these slowly in a saucepan with a little water, adding a little onion and parsley. Thicken the gravy with a little flour.

Almond Macaroons

MACARONS AUX AMANDES

	Few drops rose water
½	pound sweet almonds
½	pound white sugar
2	egg whites (not beaten)

Blanch almonds and pound them to a paste. Add a few drops of rose water to the paste. Add sugar to the egg whites. Add almond paste to the sugar mixture and work the whole together with the back of a spoon. Roll mixture in your hands in to balls about the size of a nutmeg. Place about one inch apart on buttered paper. Dust sugar over the top. Bake in a cool oven until light brown.

Frozen Champagne

Gelée au vin de Champagne (Modern version)

1	750 ml. bottle of champagne (your choice)
2	cups water
1 ½	cups sugar
½	cup lemon juice
1	cup pureed fruit of your choice (peaches, strawberries, raspberries, or kiwi)

Add sugar to water in a saucepan. Heat to a boil then reduce heat and simmer for 15–20 minutes. It will form strings when pulled with a spoon.

Cool the sugar syrup. Add all other ingredients. Pour into a plastic container and let the mixture freeze until firm.

After the mixture is firm, remove it from the freezer and pour into a bowl. Beat with an electric mixer. Return to freezer and freeze until firm.

NOTE: If preferred, this recipe can be frozen in an ice cream maker. Follow the manufacture's directions.

An engraving of Lincoln and his son, Tad, done from a photograph by Matthew Brady. The book the father and son are leafing through is a photo album that Brady had in his studio.

No family portrait was ever done of the Lincolns in their lifetimes. This engraving is an artist's rendering done in 1865, based on the above Brady photograph. Son Robert stands behind his parents. Wanting to portray all of the President's children, the artist included a portrait (seen in the upper right corner) of son Willie, who had died in February 1862.

Washington

1861 – 1865

The White House.

Illustration by Amy Castleberry.

*W*ard H. Lamon, a friend and personal body guard to the President and his family, made arrangements for the Lincolns to stay at Willard's Hotel once they arrived in Washington. On February 21, 1861, while the inaugural party was still in Philadelphia, Lamon sent a note to the proprietor of the hotel:

> *Messrs. Williard*
>
> *Gentlemen,*
>
> *We have decided after consultation with Mr. Lincoln that he, his family and party, will stop at your house. We have learned here that you were expecting us and had rooms reserved. Mr. Lincoln's family consists of himself, Mrs. Lincoln, son grown, two children, and nurse & servant.*
>
> *His private Secretary, Judge Davis & myself desire rooms adjoining Mr. Lincoln's. It is desired also that Col. Sumner, Capt. Pope, Capt. Hazzard, Mr. Judd, Mr. Hay, & Mr. Todd should have rooms as near him as possible.*
>
> *Respectfully, yours,*
> *Ward H. Lamon*[†]

After their arrival in Washington, the Lincoln family and their party stayed at Willard's until after the inauguration ceremony on March 4, 1861. They remained there for ten days, occupying Parlor 6. Dining in their room, and treating guests to champagne and cigars, they received a total bill of $773.75. Despite the cheers, toasts, and

[†] Eskew, *Willard's of Washington*, p. 51.

celebration of Lincoln becoming the new President, the city and the nation were preparing for war. Everyone experienced change. Even Willard's Hotel was preparing for the upcoming strife by "furling all sails for the storm. The dining table shorn of cartes, and the tea table reduced to the severity of pound cake."[††]

The President-elect and President James Buchanan left Willard's together the morning of the inauguration. After the ceremonies at the Capitol, Lincoln and his party returned to the hotel to watch the parade and enjoy lunch. Lincoln himself planned the simple menu that was served that afternoon. After lunch, the family went directly to the Executive Mansion.

Lincoln's Inaugural Luncheon

Mock Turtle Soup
Corned Beef and Cabbage
Parsley Potatoes
Blackberry Pie
Coffee

[††] Carr, *The Willard Hotel: An Illustrated Copy*, p. 31.

Mock Turtle Soup

Cover 5 pounds of veal bones with 14 cups water. Bring to the boiling point. Add the following ingredients, cover, and simmer for 3 ½ hours:

6	chopped celery ribs with leaves	6	crushed peppercorns
5	coarsely cut carrots	1	tablespoon salt
1	cup chopped onion	6	whole cloves
2	cups canned tomatoes	2	bay leaves
1	small can (6 ounces) tomato paste	½	teaspoon dried thyme

Remove bones and fat. In a greased skillet, sauté for five minutes 2 minced cloves of garlic, 2 pounds of ground beef, and 2 teaspoons salt. Add ¼ teaspoon Worcestershire sauce and 4 teaspoons sugar.

Add meat to the soup stock. Bring to a boil, reduce heat, and simmer 30 minutes.

Blend together 6 tablespoons of browned flour and 1 cup of cooled stock. When this has thickened to form a paste, add it to the simmering soup. Simmer for five minutes more.

Add 2 thinly sliced lemons and 1 set of chopped parboiled calf's brains.* Reheat, but do not bring to a boil.

Serve the soup garnished with 3 sliced hard-boiled eggs.

* *In Lincoln's era, a calf's head could be purchased. Instead of veal bones to make the soup stock, the calf's head was boiled, thus cooking the brains as well as making the stock. Leftover meat was picked off the bones, and the skull was then broken open to remove the cooked brains.*

Corned Beef and Cabbage

(Historic version)

Choose the thick end of a flank of beef, but do not let it be too fat. Let it lie in salt, and pickle for a week to ten days.

Sufficiently salt the meat. Prepare the following seasonings:

> One handful of parsley, chopped fine, thyme, marjoram, basil, pepper, sage (optional), allspice (optional).

Mix all well together, and cover the entire inside of the beef with the seasonings.

Roll the meat up tightly, then roll it in a clean cloth. Bind with a strong string and tie it close at the ends.

Boil it gently for three to four hours, and when cooked, take it up. Tie the ends again, quite close to the meat, and place it between two dishes with a heavy weight at the top. When it is cold, remove the cloth.

After carefully preparing the meat, it can be stored in a refrigerator for a couple of days before using.

Place meat in a deep pan. Cut green cabbage into wedges and place around meat. Cook slowly, until cabbage is tender and meat is thoroughly heated.

Corned Beef and Cabbage

(Modern version)

1   5-pound joint of corned beef
2   large onions
2   large carrots
4   potatoes
1   large cabbage
     Bay leaf
     Freshly ground black pepper

Quarter the cabbage and set aside. Peel and slice the other vegetables. Place meat in a pan with enough water to cover the meat; bring to a boil. Skim foam off the surface, add the onions, carrots, potatoes, bay leaf, and pepper and simmer gently for 90 minutes. Add the cabbage and cook for another 30 minutes. Serve the meat surrounded by the vegetables with additional cooked potatoes. Serves 4–6.

Parsley Potatoes

6   medium-sized potatoes, washed and peeled
3   tablespoons butter
3   tablespoons flour
1   cup milk
1   tablespoon parsley
     Salt and pepper to taste

Boil potatoes until tender. Drain and place in casserole dish. Melt butter in a sauce pan. Add flour and milk. Stir so flour does not lump and mixture thickens. Add parsley, salt, and pepper. Pour over potatoes. Bake in preheated 350 degree oven for 15 minutes or until hot and milk begins to bubble.

Blackberry Pie

Pastry for an 8-inch
double-crust pie
2 cups blackberries
3 tablespoons flour
¾ cup sugar
2 tablespoons butter

Preheat oven to 450 degrees. Line pie pan with unbaked pie shell. Mix together all ingredients except butter. Place berries in pie pan. Dot with butter. Either bake with a cover crust that has been vented, or with a lattice top crust. Bake for 10 minutes. Lower temperature to 375 degrees and bake for another 20–25 minutes, or till golden brown.

The President's "summer White House," the Soldiers' Home (above, as it looked about 1900), had a country rusticity that contrasted with the elegant formality of the White House in Washington.
(Both photos courtesy Abe's Antiques of Gettysburg)

White House Beverages

Sarah Josepha Hale wrote in *The Good Housekeeper* that there was one rule of domestic living that women should never violate: "Never make any preparation of which alcohol forms a part for family use!"[†] Mrs. Hale was so adamant about her position concerning alcohol that she did not allow any recipes using it in her cookbook or her domestic writings.

Mary Lincoln followed this advice as a matron in Springfield. Lincoln did not drink strong liquor. She had an older brother whose life had been destroyed by his love affair with whiskey—she was not going to serve it in her home. Even on that special night, when gentlemen came to discuss politics with Lincoln and asked him to be the Republican presidential nominee, ice water was the chosen beverage.

In the White House, Mary took a slightly different stand on the temperance issue. Although neither she nor her husband themselves partook of strong alcoholic beverages, alcohol was served at the White House. An undated telegram from Mary Lincoln requested: "Please send immediately 1 basket of Champagne, the Widow Clicquot brand. Mrs. Lincoln." Marked out at the bottom of the note was "the whole basket of your choice, quality you consider most desirable."[††] During the nineteenth century, Veuve Clicquot ("veuve" means "widow" in French) was the champagne of choice among European aristocracy. The temperance groups attacked Mary Lincoln viciously for her "lenience."

[†] Hale, Early American Cookery "The Good Housekeeper," p. 110.
[††] "Mary Lincoln Verticle File," Fort Wayne, IN.

The Lincolns were given countless bottles of imported wines, bourbons, and fine liquors. They ensured the abundant unused bottles did not go to waste. Gifts of alcohol were boxed and given to the military hospitals in the Washington area for medicinal purposes. On occasion, Mary made the deliveries to the hospital herself.

Mary Lincoln's Champagne Punch

(Makes 64 four-ounce servings)

3   quarts champagne
2   quarts sauterne
3   quarts soda water
1   gill (4 ounces) Curaçao
    Fresh fruit, such
       as strawberries,
       raspberries, peaches,
       or other fruit that is in
       season

At serving time, place a large chunk of ice in a punch bowl. Mix the liquors in another bowl, and pour into the punch bowl. Add fresh fruit to the punch and use a few pieces of fruit to adorn the top of the punch bowl.

Raspberry Shrub

(Historic 1860s version)

Pick berries when fully ripe and juicy. Place in an earthen pot which must be set into an iron pot of water. Bring the water to a boil, but take care that none of it gets into the fruit.

When the juice is extracted from the fruit, pour into a bag made of rather thick cloth which will permit the juice to pass through, but not the pulp or seeds.

Sweeten the juice to taste.

When the juice becomes perfectly clear, place a gill (4 ounces) of brandy into each bottle before pouring the juice in the bottle. Cork the bottle. Cover the cork with rosin. It will keep all summer in a cool dry place.

Raspberry Shrub

(Modern version, non-alcoholic. Makes 24 four-ounce servings)

4	packages of frozen raspberries	Cook the raspberries in a saucepan over low heat for 10 minutes. Rub berries through a strainer with a wooden spoon. Cool. Add lemonade concentrate; stir in ginger ale. Serve immediately with crushed ice.
1	can frozen lemonade concentrate	
2	quarts of ginger ale	

VARIATION: If alcohol is desired, pour a small amount of brandy or curaçao in the bottom of each cup or glass before adding the crushed ice.

Buttered Crab on Ramekins

Slices of hard cheese such as
    cheddar
Pieces of toasted bread
Crab meat
Butter

Place butter on one side of the toasted bread, and a slice of hard cheese on the other side. Grill until cheese starts to melt. Remove from the grill and spread the crab meat over the cheese. Re-grill to heat and brown the crab meat.

If desired, the toasted bread can be cut with a round cookie cutter. Then lay in a shallow muffin tray so that each ramekin forms a slight hollow into which the crab can be spooned prior to the final grilling.

Pickled Oysters

1   quart oysters in liquor
½   cup cider vinegar
1   teaspoon salt
2   blades mace
10   whole cloves
10   whole peppercorns
10   whole allspice berries
Few grains cayenne pepper

Cook the oysters in their liquor until they are plump. Remove the oysters from the liquid. Add all other ingredients to the liquid. Bring to a rolling boil and boil for five minutes.

Pour the liquid over the oysters. When cold, seal in glass jars. Store these in a cool dry place.

NOTE: This lasts for only two weeks. Do not eat them after that period.

Stewed Oysters

2   dozen oysters
1   ounce butter
    Flour
3   tablespoons milk or
        cream
    White pepper and salt to
        taste
    Parsley
    Thin strips of bread
OPTIONAL INGREDIENTS:
    Worcestershire sauce
    Grated lemon peel
    Lemon juice

Stew oysters in their own liquor. Bring to a boil and skim the liquid well. Take up oysters and beard them. Strain the liquor through a fine sieve and lay the oysters on a dish.

Put the butter in a pan and when it is melted, add just enough flour to dry up the butter. Add oyster liquor, milk, pepper, and salt. If desired, add the optional ingredients of Worcestershire sauce, lemon peel, and lemon juice at this time.

Let the liquid boil for a couple of minutes. When it is smooth, take if off the stove and add oysters. Allow the oysters to warm, but do not let them boil. Line the bottom and side of a baking dish with bread snippets. Pour oysters and sauce over the bread. Serve warm.

Oyster Stew

(Modern version)

4   tablespoons butter
1   cup milk
2   cups heavy cream
1 ½ pints oysters with liquor
Salt and pepper to taste
Dash of cayenne pepper
Chopped fresh parsley for
        garnish

Heat four bowls. Add one tablespoon of butter to each bowl and keep hot.

Heat the milk, cream, and oyster liquor to a boiling point. Add the oysters and bring the mixture to the boiling point again. Season with salt, pepper, and cayenne pepper. Place in bowls and top with parsley. Serves 4.

Tomato Bisque

2 ¼ cups chopped tomatoes
1   teaspoon sugar
3   tablespoons butter
1   bay leaf
¼   cup chopped fresh parsley
1   cup dry bread crumbs
4   cups milk (low-fat milk
        can be used)
1   small onion, chopped
        Salt and pepper to taste

In a large pot, add water just to cover the bottom of the pan. Add tomatoes and sugar and cook over medium heat for 20 minutes, or until tomatoes are tender.

In a small saucepan, melt the butter and sauté the onion until translucent. Add the onion mixture, bay leaf, and parsley to the tomatoes and cook for 5 minutes. Remove the bay leaf and discard. Puree the tomato and onion mixture. Return the mixture to the soup pot.

In a large saucepan, combine the bread crumbs and the milk; heat just to scalding. Add the milk mixture to the tomato mixture and stir well. Add salt and pepper to taste, and serve.

Mushroom Soup

1   quart water
1   pound fresh mushrooms
3   slices bacon, diced
2   tablespoons flour
2   small onion
     Juice from one can of sauerkraut (about ¼ cup)
     Salt and pepper to taste

Cook mushrooms in 1 quart water until tender. Drain; reserve liquid.

Fry bacon until partially done. Add flour; cook until lightly browned. Add onion and sauté, stirring constantly, for five minutes.

Combine sauerkraut juice with reserved mushroom liquid. Season with salt and pepper. Bring to a boil. Add ½ cup of the sauerkraut-mushroom juice mixture to bacon mixture gradually. Simmer, stirring constantly, until mixture is smooth. Add remaining liquid gradually. Add mushrooms and simmer, stirring, until well blended and heated through.

Paté de Foie Poulet

1   pound chicken livers
1 ¼ cups chicken broth
¼   medium onion
⅛   teaspoon rosemary
¼   cup softened butter
1   clove garlic (optional)
6   slices bacon, fried crisp
¼   teaspoon salt
⅛   teaspoon pepper
¼   teaspoon dry mustard

Simmer chicken livers in chicken broth for 15 minutes. Remove livers from broth, and reserve ¼ cup of the liquid. Process all ingredients except reserved broth and seasonings through a food mill; place in a bowl, add broth and seasonings and blend until well mixed. Place in a container and chill for at least 24 hours.

(Note: The modern cook may wish to combine these ingredients in a blender or food processor to save time.)

Aspic and Tongue

1	beef tongue
	Onions
	Green bell peppers
¼	cup cherry juice
	Aspic

Preheat oven to 200 degrees. Place tongue in a pan with water with onions and peppers and bake for six hours. Add cherry juice and continue cooking until tongue is tender. Let cool, slice, and arrange on a cool tray; cover with aspic and serve.

NOTE: Aspic is clear gelatin made from meat. Place the meat in two quarts of cold water. Bring to a boil, skim foam from the top, then reduce heat and simmer for six hours. Remove meat, strain the broth into a deep dish, and refrigerate for at least 24 hours. Remove the fat from the top, bring broth to a boil, and reduce to about one quart. For all practical, modern purposes, unflavored gelatin is quicker, easier, and produces almost the same results. Prepare it with a meat stock instead of water.

Smoked Venison with Applesauce

Smoke a venison roast in a smoker with the meat over a pan of water and fruit juice that is available as per season. Pack fruit around the meat to keep it moist. Use a good fruit wood or hickory wood for the smoke. Keep the pan from going dry by adding water whenever needed. When the meat is judged to be cooked, slice it and let it cool. Serve the venison cold with applesauce in small portions.

Chicken Salad

Chicken, cut up
Celery
Mayonnaise
Hard-boiled eggs
Lettuce leaves
Celery tips
Cold, boiled beets
Olives

Boil the meat until tender and thoroughly cooked. Remove all the fat, gristle and skin. Mince the meat into small pieces, but do not hash it.

For every cup of chicken meat, use 2 ½ cups of celery that has been cut into pieces about one-quarter of an inch thick. Use enough mayonnaise to coat the ingredients. Garnish with your choice of hard-boiled eggs, lettuce leaves, celery tips, beets, and olives.

Note: Turkey salad can be made in the same fashion.

Lobster Salad

Lobster
French dressing
Mayonnaise
Capers
Parsley
Lettuce leaves

Boil lobster until done. When cool, pick all of the meat from the shell. Mince the lobster meat.

Mix together equal parts of French dressing and mayonnaise.

Make a nest with each lettuce leaf. Place a large spoonful of the minced lobster meat on each lettuce leaf. Put the dressing on top of the lobster. Garnish with caper sprinkled over the dress and parsley sprinkled around each leaf. Serve cold.

Caraway Bread

2	packages of yeast
¾	cup warm water
1 ¼	cups buttermilk or sour milk
5	cups flour (about)
¼	cup shortening
2	tablespoons sugar
2	teaspoons baking powder
2	teaspoons salt
1	tablespoon caraway seeds
	Soft butter

Dissolve yeast in warm water in a large bowl. Add buttermilk, 2 ½ cups flour, shortening, sugar, baking powder, salt, and caraway seeds. Blend for 30 seconds at low speed with an electric mixer, or for about 1 minute by hand. Scrap sides and bottom of the bowl while mixing. Beat for two minutes at medium speed with an electric mixer, or beat rigorously by hand. Stir in remaining flour by hand. Dough should be soft and slightly sticky.

Turn dough onto heavily floured board; knead well. Roll dough to 18 by 9-inch rectangle. Roll up from short side as for jelly roll; press each end to seal. Fold ends under loaf. Place seam-side down in a greased bread pan; brush loaf lightly with butter. Let rise for 1 hour, or until double in bulk. Bake at 375 degrees for 45 minutes or until bread tests done.

Corn Bread

¾   cup sifted flour
1 ¼   cups corn meal
4   teaspoons baking powder
1   teaspoon salt
2   tablespoons sugar
2   eggs, well beaten
1 ¼   cups milk
¼   cup melted butter

Combine dry ingredients. Combine eggs and milk and add to flour mixture, stirring until well mixed. Add melted butter. Turn into a greased, shallow pan, or into corn muffin tins. Bake at 400 degrees for 30 minutes.

(NOTE: Sugar may be omitted if desired.)

Weisskohl mit Speck

CABBAGE WITH BACON

1   medium head of white cabbage (about 1 ½ pounds) finely shredded
4   slices bacon
¼   cup vinegar
1   teaspoon sugar
½   teaspoon dry mustard
¼   teaspoon salt
⅛   teaspoon pepper
5   green onions with tops, sliced (about ½ cup)

Cover cabbage with boiling water in a 4-quart bowl. Let stand for 10 minutes; drain. Cook bacon in a large skillet until crisp. Remove from heat. Crumble the bacon into small pieces. Add vinegar, sugar, mustard, salt and pepper; heat thoroughly over medium heat. Add the cabbage and onions. Toss until cabbage is coated with the bacon mixture. Serves 6.

Colorful pieces adorned the White House table during the Lincolns' time there, such as this Dorflinger cut crystal goblet and a plate trimmed in gold and *solferino* (a purplish-red). The plate, which has been restored, was part of the official White House china.

(Photos 4645 [goblet] and 4644 [plate] courtesy of the Collection of Lincoln Financial Foundation, Fort Wayne, IN.)

This soup tureen is part of a set of china Mary Lincoln purchased for her personal use in Washington.

(Courtesy of Abraham Lincoln Presidential Library and Museum, Springfield, IL.)

Asian-style florals
decorated the elegant
teaset used by the
Lincolns in Springfield.
(Both photos courtesy of Abraham
Lincoln Library and Museum,
Harrogate, TN.)

This white dish with a
delicate border of violets
was among the pieces
used by the Lincolns in
Springfield.
(Photo LR374; courtesy of Abraham
Lincoln Presidential Library and Museum,
Springfield, IL.)

Delmonico's Restaurant was a favorite dining haunt of the President's when he was in New York City. During one visit Lincoln told the owner, Lorenzo Delmonico, "In my city of Washington there are many mansions, but alas, we have no cooks like yours."

Delmonico Potatoes

4	medium potatoes
¾	cup milk
¼	cup heavy whipping cream
½	teaspoon salt
¼	teaspoon white pepper
¼	teaspoon freshly grated nutmeg
2	tablespoons grated Parmesan cheese

Wash but do not skin the potatoes. Quarter them lengthwise. Bring 8 cups water to a boil and add potatoes. Let boil for 10 minutes so that the potatoes are not cooked through. Immediately submerge the hot potatoes in cold water, and let them cool for 30 minutes. Grate into long strips.

Mix together milk, cream, salt, pepper, and nutmeg.

Preheat a large frying pan over medium heat and then add potatoes and liquid mixture. Fold them together well, but gently. Cook for 10 minutes, mixing lightly so they do not burn.

Remove from the heat and fold in 1 tablespoon cheese. Transfer into a buttered baking dish and arrange evenly. Sprinkle remaining cheese on top.

Preheat oven to 425. Place uncovered dish in the upper third of the oven and bake for 6 minutes or until lightly browned.

Maple Glazed Turnips

1   pound sliced young
    turnips
3   tablespoons brown sugar
    Maple syrup
    Butter

Steam turnips in a small among of water in a steamer for 20 minutes or until tender. Drain. Season with brown sugar, maple syrup, and butter. Toss lightly

Beef à la Mode

Cut several holes in a piece of round roast, weighing about six pounds. Fill the holes with stuffing (recipe follows). Bind wide strips of clean cloth over the cuts to keep the stuffing inside.

After the beef has been stuffed, lay it on skewers in a roasting pan. Pour 3 pints of boiling water over the roast, and cover the pan tightly with its lid. Stew the meat in a moderate oven (350 degrees) for about four hours. When done, take it up and remove the cloth. Keep the meat hot.

Remove the skewers from the pan and thicken the gravy with 1 tablespoon of flour. Mix smoothly with a little gravy and boil for one minute. Season with salt and pepper and 3 tablespoons of tomato catsup.

STUFFING INGREDIENTS:
¾   pound raw beef
¼   pound fat salt pork
1   pound grated bread
¼   pound butter
1   teaspoon each of thyme, savory, cloves, and allspice
2   teaspoon salt
1   teaspoon pepper
    Dash of cayenne pepper

Filet of Beef

1   small beef shoulder,
       rump, or chuck roast
1   tablespoon
       Worcestershire sauce
1   cup red wine
    Pepper to taste
¼   teaspoon tarragon
¼   teaspoon rosemary
1   small onion, sliced

Preheat oven to 300 degrees. Place beef in a lidded roasting pan. Mix all other ingredients together and pour over the top of the beef. Cover and roast until meat is done, turning occasionally. (Roasting time will vary, depending on the size of the roast.)

Wine-Glazed Ham

1   10-pound ham
    Whole cloves
2 ½ cups white wine
1   cup honey
1   cup brown sugar, packed

Remove rind from ham, leaving a thin layer of fat. Score the fat. Stud with cloves. Place, fat-side up, in a roaster. Pour white wine over the ham. Spread honey over top; sprinkle with brown sugar. Bake at 300 degrees for 1 hour. Cover; bake for 3 hours longer or until ham is tender, basting frequently.

The President's Chaire

1	chicken (3 to 3 ½ pounds)
1	cup water
¼	cup lemon juice
1	onion, chopped
	Salt and pepper to taste
3	tablespoons prepared mustard
2	tablespoons brown sugar
2	teaspoons fat
½	cup chopped celery
1	cup catsup
2	tablespoons vinegar

Cut chicken into serving pieces. Brown in hot fat in a skillet. Remove chicken pieces and place in a casserole dish. Add chopped onion to fat and brown lightly. Add remaining ingredients and simmer for 30 minutes. Pour over browned chicken in the casserole. Cover casserole with a dome shaped lid and bake at 350 degrees for one hour. Serves 6–8.

Roast Goose with Apricot Stuffing

2 ¼	cups cooked unsweetened apricots
2	cups fresh bread crumbs
¼	cup butter, melted
¼	cup slivered, toasted almonds
	Pepper to taste
2	cups cracker crumbs
¼	cup minced celery
1 ¼	teaspoons salt
1	goose

Cut apricots into small pieces. Add remaining ingredients and stir well.

Preheat oven to 375 degrees. Stuff goose with apricot mixture. Truss and place breast down in a large roasting pan. Pour 2 cups of boiling water over the goose and cover the pan with lid. Bake 30 minutes. Turn goose breast up and prick with a fork in inconspicuous places about the legs and wings, so that the fat will run out. Reduce heat to 300 degrees and roast for 2–2 ¼ hours, adding more water as necessary. Remove lid and roast uncovered for another 15 minutes to brown.

Boned Turkey

(This is a very difficult dish and should only be attempted by the most skilled hands)

Clean the fowl as usual with a sharp and pointed knife. Begin at the extremity of the wing and pass the knife down close to the bone, cutting all the flesh from the bone, and preserving the skin whole. Run the knife down each side of the breast bone and up the legs, keeping close to the bone. Split the back half way up, and draw out the bones.

Fill the places where the bones had been with a stuffing, restoring the fowl to its natural shape and sew up all the incisions made in the skin.

Lard the meat with two or three rows of fatty bacon on top of the turkey breast. Place in a roasting pan and roast on medium heat (325–350 degrees) until turkey is well done and stuffing has reached an internal temperature of 165 degrees. Use a meat thermometer to determine the internal temperature.

While cooking, baste often with salt, water, and a little butter.

When done, carve across in slices and serve with tomato sauce if desired.

STUFFING OPTION 1:

1	loaf stale bread
½	pound butter
1	whole nutmeg
	Salt and pepper to taste
2	eggs
	Mixture of sweet herbs

Mix well until very smooth. Stuff into turkey cavity, or bake separately in a baking dish.

STUFFING OPTION 2:

	Equal parts of stale bread and corn bread
	Pecan nuts
	Truffles
1	egg
	Mixture of sweet herbs
	Salt and pepper to taste

Mix well until smooth. Stuff into turkey cavity, or bake separately in a baking dish.

APPROXIMATE COOKING TIMES FOR TURKEY

UNSTUFFED

4–6 lb breast..	1 ½–2 ¼ hrs
6–8 lb breast..	2 ¼–3 ¼ hrs
8–12 lbs	.2 ¾–3 hrs
12–14 lbs	.3–3 ¾ hrs
14–18 lbs	.3 ¾–4 ¼ hrs
18–20 lbs	.4 ¼–4 ½ hrs
20–24 lbs	.4 ½–5 hrs

STUFFED

8–12 lbs	.3–3 ½ hrs
12–14 lbs	.3 ½–4 hrs
14–18 lbs	.4–4 ¼ hrs
18–20 lbs	.4 ¼–4 ¾ hrs
20–24 lbs	.4 ¾–5 ¼ hrs

Stuffed Turkey with Truffles

1   pound truffles
Small turkey
Bacon fat
Salt and pepper to taste

Keep the finest truffles whole, and chop the others very fine. Chop or pound in a mortar the white fat of bacon until you have equal amounts of fat and truffles. Mix the bacon fat and truffles together. Season with salt and pepper.

Stuff the turkey with the truffle mixture. Sew up the fowl and truss it. Keep it in the refrigerator for a day or two.

Roast or bake carefully saving all the drippings for sauces and gravies.

Almond Sponge Cake

(Historic White House version)

1	pint fine flour
2	heaping teaspoonfuls baking powder
2	ounces of sweet almonds
2	ounces of bitter almonds
10	eggs, separated
2	cups powdered sugar

Sift flour and baking powder together; set aside. Blanch the almonds in scalding water, renewing the hot water when expedient. When the skins are completely removed, wash the almonds in cold water and wipe them dry. Pound the almonds, one at a time, into a fine, smooth paste, adding water or a little egg white to prevent their boiling if necessary. Set them in a cool place.

Separate the eggs and beat the whites and yolks separately until very smooth and thick. Gradually beat the eggs into the powdered sugar, and alternate adding the eggs with the pounded almond paste. Lastly add the flour mixture. Stir it slowly in circles and lightly on the surface of the mixture, as is done in common sponge cake.

Bake in a buttered deep square pan. Carefully place the mixture into the pan and set it into a moderate oven. Bake until thoroughly done and risen very high, about 45 minutes. When cool, cover it with plain white icing that has been flavored with rose water or with a little almond extract.

Sponge Cake

(Historic version)

4	egg yolks
2	cups fine powdered sugar
1	cup sifted flour
4	egg whites, beaten stiff
1	cup sifted flour
2	teaspoons baking powder
1	scant teacup of boiling water
	Flavoring of choice (vanilla extract, lemon extract)
	Pinch of salt

Sift one cup of flour and baking powder together. Set aside.

Beat the egg yolks together. Add powdered sugar. Gradually add one cup of sifted flour. Fold in egg whites.

Add flour with the baking powder, and the teacup of boiling water a little at a time. Add flavoring and salt. However thin the mixture may seem, do not add any more flour.

Pour into prepared shallow tins and bake in a moderate oven (350 degrees) for 15 minutes or until cake tests done.

Lady Cake

(Historic version)

As with many historic recipes, this one does not give complete baking instructions. A moderate oven (350) is suggested. The cake should be checked frequently and baked until it tests done.

1	pound flour
1	pound sugar
⅝	pound butter
17	egg whites
2	or 3 drops of bitter almond oil

Cream the butter. Add the sugar and cream again. Slowly add flour. Add the flavoring. Beat egg whites to form stiff peaks and gently fold into batter.

Pour into a prepared square or long pan and bake in a moderate oven until done.

Fancy Cakes

(Historic White House version)

These delicious little fancy cakes may be made by making a rich jumble paste—rolling out in any desired shape. Cut some of the paste in thick, narrow strips and lay around your cakes, so as to form a deep, cup-like edge. Place on a well buttered tin and bake. When done, fill with iced fruit, prepared as follows:

Take rich, ripe peaches cut in halves; plums, strawberries, pineapples cut in squares or small triangles, or any other available fruit and dip in the white of an egg that has been very slightly beaten and then place the fruit in pulverized sugar. Lay the fruit in the center of your cakes.

MODERN HELPFUL HINTS: A jumble paste is cookie dough that has grated citrus peel added to it. For Fancy Cakes, make a basic sugar cookie or molding cookie dough, adding grated citrus peel to it. Form cookies with an indented center and bake until done. While cookies are still warm, fill the centers with fruit that has been prepared in the same manner as the historic version of the recipe.

Pound Cake

(Historic version)

This cake can be kept for a few weeks if stored properly. Nineteenth-century cooks placed the cake in an earthen jar. They then soaked a piece of letter paper in brandy and placed that over the top of the cake. The jar was then covered with a lid.

1	pound butter
1	pound sugar
12	egg yolks
1	whole nutmeg, grated
1	glass wine or rose water
12	egg whites

Beat butter to a cream. Add sugar and mix well. Beat the egg yolks and add to the butter and sugar mixture. Mix well. Add nutmeg and wine or rose water. Stir in flour. Beat egg whites until stiff and fold into batter.

Pour out into a large, prepared cake pan and bake until a nice light brown.

This could also be divided and baked in pound cake loaf pans. Bake in a moderate oven (350 degrees) for about an hour.

Berries in Filled Dough

Pie pastry dough

FILLING:

1	cup butter
4	eggs
2	cups sugar
1	teaspoon vanilla

TOPPING:

	Raspberries and blueberries
2	cups whipped cream
	Powdered sugar

FOR THE PASTRY: Roll pastry dough thinly and cut into circles to fit into individual baking cups.

FOR THE FILLING: Preheat oven to 375 degrees. Combine ingredients and pour into pastry cups. Bake for 10 minutes or until light brown.

FOR THE TOPPING: Remove pastries from cups. Top with berries, powdered sugar and whipped cream.

Dame Blanche

¾	cup plus 2 tablespoons unsalted butter, cold and cubed	2	large eggs	
		1	vanilla bean	
½	cup almond flour (or cornstarch)	1	cup cake flour	
		1	cup all-purpose flour	
¾	cup plus 2 tablespoons powdered sugar		Pinch of salt	
		½	cup raspberry jam	
		¼	cup powdered sugar	

Place butter, almond flour, and sugar in a large mixing bowl. Mix on medium speed adding eggs one at a time. Mix until batter resembles scrambled eggs.

Using a sharp knife, slice the vanilla bean in half lengthwise. Separate the seeds from the bean by scraping the knife blade along the inside of the bean.

Add the vanilla bean seeds, flour, and salt to the butter mixture. Mix on medium speed for about one minute. Do not over beat the dough.

Place the dough on a lightly floured work surface and pat into a rectangle shape. Wrap in plastic wrap and refrigerate for at least 30 minutes. This dough can be refrigerated overnight if desired.

When ready to bake the cookies, roll the dough about 1/8 inch thick. Using a 2 1/2-inch wide heart shaped cookie cutter, stamp out as many cookies as possible. Pat together any left over dough and roll it out. Place cookies 1 inch apart on a parchment covered baking sheet. Use a sharp knife or a top of a plain decorate tip to cut the centers from half of the cookies. Make the opening the shape of a heart. The dough from the opening can be used to make more cookies. Just be sure to have an equal number of those with and without the cut out.

Bake until golden brown, about 10 minutes at 350 degrees. Remove from the oven and place on a wire rack. Cool completely. Spread a think layer of jam on top of the cookies without the cutout. Do not cover completely with jam—leave about a ¼-inch border. These are the bottom cookies. Sprinkle the cut out cookies with powdered sugar through a fine mesh sieve. Sandwich the cut out cookies on top of the bottoms.

Makes 2–2 ½ dozen cookies. These should be stored in an airtight container. They keep 4–5 days.

Macaroon Tarts

Pie dough
Preserves (choice of
  flavor)
3 egg whites
½ pound powdered sugar
½ pound grated almonds

Line a muffin pan with rich pie dough. Fill half of each muffin well with any desired flavor of preserves and bake in a quick oven for 20–25 minutes. Check often.

Beat the egg whites to a stiff froth and slowly add powdered sugar. Stir about 10 minutes (by hand) until very light. If using an electric mixer, chill both the bowl and the blades so the mixture does not get too warm. Mix on medium-high speed for about 4 minutes. Gradually fold in almonds. It will form a paste.

Divide the paste into equal portions. Roll and shape into strips, dusting hands with powdered sugar to prevent the paste from sticking. Place the strips in parallel rows across the tops of the baked tarts. Place the next row of strips diagonally across the first row. Reduce the oven temperature to a slow oven (about 250 degrees) and make for 15 minutes.

After baking, leave the tarts in the pans until they are almost cold.

Chocolate Pie

MERINGUE CRUST *(for a large pie pan or 2 small ones)*:

3   egg whites
¼   teaspoon cream of tartar
¾   cup sugar

FILLING:

1   cup butter
4   eggs
2   cups sugar
1   teaspoon vanilla

HOT FUDGE SAUCE:
    (makes 1–1 ¾ cups)

¾   cup sugar
½   cup cocoa
1   5-ounce can evaporated milk
⅓   cup light corn syrup
⅓   cup butter
1   teaspoon vanilla

FOR THE CRUST: Beat egg whites until soft peaks form. Slowly add other ingredients. Beat until stiff peaks form as for a meringue. Gently spoon into pie pan. Bake at 275 degrees for one hour.

FOR THE FILLING: Combine ingredients and beat for 20 minutes. Gently pour into meringue crust. Bake at 375 degrees for 10 minutes. Garnish with hot fudge sauce.

FOR THE SAUCE: Combine sugar and cocoa in a medium saucepan. Stir in evaporated milk and corn syrup. Cook over medium heat, stirring constantly until the mixture boils. Boil for 1 minute. Remove from heat. Stir in butter and vanilla. Serve warm over above pie or other desserts.

A receipt book of a Washington baker records that President Lincoln was a steady customer for this unusually rich pecan pie.

Molasses Pecan Pie

3	eggs
¾	cup unsulphured molasses
¾	cup white corn syrup
1	teaspoon vanilla extract
1	tablespoon flour
2	tablespoons melted butter
⅛	teaspoon salt
1	cup chopped pecans
1	unbaked 8-inch pie shell

Preheat oven to 375 degrees. Beat eggs until light and frothy. Add melted butter; mix well. Add molasses, white corn syrup, salt, and vanilla. Mix well. Coat the pecans with the flour; then add floured nuts to the egg-butter mixture. Mix thoroughly and pour into pie shell. Bake for 40 minutes or until the filling sets and becomes firm.

As a child in New Hampshire, nineteenth-century author Sarah Josepha Hale and her family had celebrated Thanksgiving Day, a common practice only in some states. She began a lifelong crusade to have Thanksgiving Day declared a national holiday. In 1863, when she was seventy-five years old, President Abraham Lincoln made her dream a reality. He wrote:

> *[I] invite my fellow citizens in every part of the United States, and also those who are at sea, or who are sojourning in foreign lands, to set apart and observe the last Thursday of November next as a day of thanksgiving and praise to our Beneficent Father.[†]*

---

† Basler, *Collective Works of Abraham Lincoln 1809–1865*, Vol. 6, p. 497.

Pumpkin Pie

1 ½   cups cooked pumpkin
3   eggs, separated
1 ½   cups scalded milk
2   tablespoons butter
½   teaspoon salt
1   teaspoon cinnamon
1   cup sugar
½   teaspoon ginger
¼   teaspoon nutmeg
1   unbaked 9-inch pie shell

Strain the cooked pumpkin. Lightly beat the egg yolks and add to the pumpkin.

Melt butter in hot milk. Add scalded milk to pumpkin mixture. Mix well. Add sugar, salt, ginger, cinnamon, and nutmeg. Mix thoroughly.

Beat egg whites until stiff peaks form. Carefully fold egg whites into pumpkin mixture. Pour mixture into unbaked pie shell. Bake in a preheated 450 degree oven for 10 minutes. Reduce heat to 350 degrees and bake for 20–25 minutes longer. When a knife can be inserted into the filling and it comes out clean, the pie is done.

Rich Pumpkin Pie

10   eggs
4   cups cooked, strained
         pumpkin
2   cups dark brown sugar
1   teaspoon mace
1   tablespoon brandy
½   teaspoon nutmeg
1   teaspoon cinnamon
1 ¼   quarts whole milk
2   unbaked 9-inch pie shells

Separate the eggs. Beat the 10 egg yolks and combine with the pumpkin in a large bowl. Add brown sugar and spices. Mix well. Add brandy. Mix again. Slowly add the milk, beating well as it is added.

Beat the 10 egg whites until stiff peaks form. Fold into the pumpkin mixture.

Pour mixture into pie shells. Bake for 20 minutes in a 425 degree oven. Reduce heat to 325 degrees and bake another 25 minutes or until center is firm.

Sicilian Sorbet

Fresh peaches
2 cups orange juice
1 cup sugar
2 tablespoons lemon juice

Press the peaches through a sieve. Add sugar and juices. Freeze and serve.

Blanc Mangue

2 ounces unflavored gelatin
Cold water
2 quarts rich milk
1 teacupful fine white sugar
Flavor to taste with
    lemon, vanilla, or
    peach water
Fresh fruit

Dissolve gelatin in cold water. When it is thoroughly dissolved, stir it into the milk. Add sugar and flavoring. Place mixture on stove top and bring to a boil, stirring continually. Let it boil for five minutes. Strain mixture through a cloth, and pour into molds which have been previously wet with cold water and salt. Let it stand on ice (or in the freezer) until it becomes hard and cold. Turn it out carefully upon dishes and serve.

Or, fill half of the mold and freezer this portion hard. Then add cherries, peaches, strawberries, or sliced bananas as you chose. Add remaining cream and freeze hard. Turn out carefully and serve.

Biscuit Glace

During the nineteenth century, ice cream and sherbet were often served in small, fancy paper cases.

Make and freeze the cream; then fill the paper cases with two kinds of cream—either sherbet or plain ice cream with tutti-frutti—Charlotte Russe cream with sherbet or ice cream.

Pack cases in a freezer and keep on ice and salt until very hard. Serve on a lace paper napkin that is laid on a fancy plate. Sometimes, these are covered with a meringue and colored slightly just before serving.

To make the cream:

1	pint rich ream
⅓	cup sugar
1	teaspoon vanilla extract

Mix together in a deep bowl, cream, sugar, and vanilla extract. Put the mixture in a cold pan and whip to a stiff froth. Stir this down and whip again. Skim the froth into a deep dish. When all of the cream has been whipped to froth, fill the paper cases and place in the freezer. Freeze for two hours.

Make a pint of sherbet. Place a thin layer of sherbet on each case of cream and return to freezer. Freeze for half an hour or longer and serve.

Note: Paper cases are difficult, if not impossible to find in the modern marketplace. The closest available modern items are the paper cases used in individual ice cream treats such as "Push-ups." For the person making this recipe at home, a ceramic dish, individual mold, or even a Popsicle mold can be used.

Chocolate Bavarian Cream

1	pint cream
1	cup milk
½	cup sugar
½	box unflavored gelatin
1	ounce square baking chocolate
1	tablespoon hot water

Soak gelatin in ½ cup of the milk. Set aside. Whip cream to a stiff froth and set aside.

Scrape the chocolate, and add two tablespoons sugar to it. Put in a small frying pan with hot water. Stir over hot heat until chocolate is melted and mixture is smooth and glossy.

Have the remaining ½ cup of milk boiling. Stir in the chocolate. Add gelatin mixture.

Strain into a tin basin and add remaining sugar. Place the basin in a pan of ice water and beat the mixture until it begins to thicken. Add whipped cream.

Mix well, turn into a mold. Chill until firm and turn out onto a serving plate. Serve with whipped cream heaped around.

Mary Lincoln, 1861.

The accepted method of White House entertaining during the winter months was weekly, public receptions where anyone who wished to attend could do so and shake hands with the President. By the end of 1861, thousands of people had moved into Washington for military operations and the war effort, and they often looked for some form of free entertainment. The city, however, was overflowing with people, and public gatherings of any kind often suffered from a lack of crowd control. The White House receptions were no different as they often drew crowds of three thousand or more people. Lincoln often commented that his hand was swollen from shaking hands with so many guests. But public receptions were tradition, and tradition in any social sphere is difficult to break. According to one reporter, public receptions began due to "a false deference to the false notion of democratic equality which certainly is practiced by no private family, however humble, and which no one has a right to exact from that of the President."[†]

Mary Lincoln decided to change this standing tradition and hold a party instead. She had just finished the extensive renovations for the Executive Mansion, and a party would be an excellent way for Mary to reveal the exquisite new décor to Washington society. She issued engraved invitations for the evening of February 5, 1862, to six or seven hundred select persons. Lincoln's secretary, John Nicolay, explained the cards caused equal amounts of "decided sensation" and disappointment when he wrote, "Half the city is jubilant at being invited, while the other half is furious at being left out in the cold."[††]

[†] *Frank Leslie's Illustrated Newspaper*, February 22, 1862, p. 209, col. 1.

[††] Bernard, "Lincoln and the Music of the Civil War, VIII."

Guests began arriving at 9 P.M. When they entered the White House, they were greeted by doormen wearing solferino-colored coats that matched the trim on the new White House china. Guests were escorted to the second story where rooms had been set open for dressing rooms. Soon, they entered the newly refurbished East Room. The Green, Red, and Blue rooms were all "richly decorated with a profusion of natural flowers."††† Music was provided by the Marine Band under the direction of Francis Scala. For the evening, he composed a special musical tribute for Mary titled "Mary Lincoln Polka."

A midnight supper prepared by Mr. Maillard and Company of New York awaited the guests in the dining room. The caterer had "provided nearly a ton of turkeys, ducks, venison, pheasants, partridges, hams, and delicacies, such as stewed and scalloped oysters, Charlotte Russe à la Parisienne, orange glace, fancy cakes, fruits, and grapes."†††† Newspapers across the country reported the dinner was "one of the finest displays of gastronomic art ever seen in this country" and that it had been prepared "at a cost of thousands of dollars."††††† However, check records show on March 1, Lincoln wrote a check for $1,060.91. It is assumed by most historians this check was payment for the caterer.

Although the party was considered a social success, on a personal level the Lincolns were far from jubilant. Their son Willie lay upstairs, ill with fever and his parents spent much of the evening at his bedside. Tragically, the boy died several days later.

---

††† Ibid.

†††† Ibid.

††††† *New Orleans Daily Delta*, April 9, 1862, and the *National Telegraph*, Clarksburg, W. Va., Feb. 14, 1862.

Decorations
& Candy Ornaments Included:

A five-foot-high vase, filled with natural flowers, wreaths of which gracefully vined about the sides and base of the vase.

A United States steam frigate of forty guns, with all sail set, and the flag of the Union flying at the main.

A representation of the Hermitage.

A Warrior's helmet, supported by Cupids.

A Chinese pagoda.

Double cornucopias, resting upon a shell, supported by mermaids, surmounted by a crystal star.

A rustic pavilion.

The Goddess of Liberty.

A magnificent candelabra, surmounted by an elegant vase of flowers and surrounded by tropical fruits and birds, tastefully arranged and sustained by kneeling Cupids.

A basket, laden with flowers and fruits, mounted on a pedestal supported by swans.

Four bee hives.

A Swiss cottage in sugar and cake.

A large fort, named Fort Pickens, made of cake and sugar. The inside was filled with quails, candied.

Menu for a White House Party

February 5, 1862

Stewed Oysters

Scalloped Oysters

Boned Turkey

Paté de Foie Gras

Aspic of Torgul

Patti-Gillets, à la Fanisanz

Chicken Salad, à la Parisenne

Filet of Beef

Stuffed Turkey with Truffles

Quails

Canvas Back Ducks

Charlotte Russe, à la Parisenne

Chateaubriand

Chocolate Bavarian

Jelly Compettes

Fruit Glacé

Bon-Bons

Orange Glacé

Biscuit Glacé

Fancy Cakes

Sandwiches

Fruit and Grapes

Meringues

The East Ballroom
as it appeared during
Lincoln's time.
(Courtesy Abe's Antiques of Gettysburg)

Bill of Fare
OF THE
Presidential Inauguration Ball
IN THE
CITY OF WASHINGTON, D.C.
ON THE 6TH OF MARCH 1865.

Oyster Stew......

Terrapin Stew......

Oysters, pickled ......

BEEF,
Roast Beef......

Filet of Beef......

Beef à la mode......

Beef à l'anglais......

VEAL,
Leg of Veal......

Fricandeau......

Veal Malakoff......

POULTRY,
Roast Turkey......

Boned Turkey......

Breast Chicken......

Grouse, boned and roast ......

GAME,
Pheasant......

Quail ......

Venison......

PATETES,
Patète of Duck en gelee

Patète de Foie gras......

SMOKED,
Ham ......

Tongue en gelée ......

do plain......

SALADES,
Chicken ......

Lobster......

ORNAMENTAL PYRAMIDES,
Nougate ......

Orange......

Caramel with Fancy Cream Candy......

Cocoanut......

Macaroon......

Croquant ......

Chocolates......

Trea Cakes......

CAKES AND TARTS,
Almond Sponge......

Belle Alliance......

Dame Blanche......

Macaroon Tart......

Tart à la Nelson......

Tart à l'Orleans......

do à la Portugaise......

do à la Vienne......

Pound Cake......

Sponge Cake......

Lady Cake......

Fancy small cakes ......

JELLIES AND CREAMS,
Calf's foot and Wine Jelly......

Charlotte à la Russe......

do du Vanilla......

Blanc Mangue ......

Crème Neapolitano......

do à la Nelson......

do Chateaubriand......

do à la Smyrna......

do à la Nesselrode......

Bombe à la Vanilla......

ICE CREAM,
Vanilla......

Lemon......

White Coffee......

Chocolate......

Burnt Almond......

Maraschino ......

FRUIT ICES,
Strawberry......

Orange......

Lemon......

DESSERT,
Grapes, Almonds, Raisins, &c

Coffee and Chocolate

Furnished by G. A. BALZER, Confectioners,
Cor. 9th & D Sts, Washington, D.C.

(Menu courtesy of the Lincoln Boyhood National Historic Site)

One of the last photographs of Abraham Lincoln was taken by subterfuge on March 6, 1865, two days after Lincoln gave his second inaugural address. Henry F. Warren, a photographer unknown to the President, managed to get into the White House grounds, where he found young Tad Lincoln and offered to photograph the child on his pony if he would get his father to pose also. The ruse was successful, and Tad coaxed his father to come out on the balcony for the photographer. It is speculated that Lincoln's annoyance with Warren's trick was the cause of his stern expression—or perhaps it was the wind that whipped his hair and possibly stung his eyes. Abraham Lincoln was assassinated less than six weeks later. (Author's collection.)

Epilogue

Often the question is asked: What did Lincoln eat for his last meal before going to Ford's Theatre?

One envisions a grand supper consisting of several courses served on elegant china in the White House dining room. Perhaps he enjoyed some of his favorites such as oysters or fricasseed chicken. He may have savored a piece of molasses pecan pie for dessert or indulged in an extra piece of pound cake and ice cream.

But this is not the answer to the question, because despite what we would like to believe or imagine, the answer is simply that the only thing recorded about his last dinner is that it was cold.

The last day of Lincoln's life was busy. Robert Lincoln was home at the White House that morning and had breakfast with his father. After the President entered his office, the morning was filled with appointments, interviews, and paperwork. He made a quick trip to the War Department searching for the latest news from the troops, then headed back to the White House for a cabinet meeting. One historian noted that Lincoln was too busy for lunch and ate an apple on his way back to his office.[§] The afternoon schedule was much the same as his morning schedule, full of appointments and interviews.

Later in the afternoon, Lincoln and his wife enjoyed a carriage ride. Mary later described the President's mood as "supremely cheerful—his manner was even playful."[§§] When they returned from the carriage ride, friends from Illinois, Governor Richard J. Oglesby

[§] Donald, *Lincoln*, p. 593.
[§§] Turner and Turner, *Mary Todd Lincoln: Her Life and Letters*, p. 284.

LINCOLN IN THE SUMMER OF 1860.

and General Isham Haynie were waiting at the White House. Lincoln chatted with them and read so many chapters of the *Nasby Letters*[†] that dinner was waiting to be served. Several times, someone was sent to summon Lincoln to the table. Finally, he came to dinner to eat what would become is last meal. There exists a traditional belief that Lincoln dined on cold meat and potatoes that evening. Whether the meal was cold by design (such as a nice turkey sandwich and potato salad) or cold from his tardiness has not really been determined. Whatever his meal consisted of was most likely eaten in a hurry. The President and his lady were late for the theatre. And when they arrived, the play was already in progress.

† Petroleum Vesuvius Nasby was the pseudonym of David Ross Locke, an American journalist, humorist, and political commentator during the mid-nineteenth century. Locke used a series of letters written by Nasby to encourage readers to support the Union cause. Lincoln was a fan of the letters; read them frequently; and often quoted from them.

The two engravings (above) show Mary Lincoln in 1864. The photo at left was taken in 1861.
(All photos, author's collection)

Acknowledgments

Any historical work begins with research. Looking for references to food and menus requires searching of many personal records: Old letters give insight into what was served at various family occasions; diaries often mention a special dinner or dish. Newspapers sometimes give details about what was served at a social or White House function. Old cookbooks provide recipes and sometimes menus. Documents such as these are found at historic sites and libraries. I am deeply grateful to the many people at these sites for assisting with information and validation of the stories about Lincoln family members and their life style.

The first edition of *Lincoln's Table* mentions several people at historic sites who are no longer employed by those organizations. Staff members at Farmington, Abraham Lincoln Birthplace National Historic Site, Lincoln Boyhood Memorial, The Lincoln Home National Historic Site, Mary Todd Lincoln House, and Willard's Intercontinental Hotel all assisted with the first edition. Even though those individuals have move to other positions, I still am grateful for their help. They know who they are.

The Abraham Lincoln Presidential Museum and Library has opened since the first edition was published in December 2000. Many people who work there have helped me find the needed tidbits and historical documentation for this edition: Jane Ehrenhart, Jennifer Ericson, Kathryn M. Harris, and Dr. James M. Cornelius all gave assistance and guidance for finding wonderful stories about the Lincolns and Springfield.

Sometimes, the source of a particular story is difficult to track down. A very special thank you goes to the staff at the Stephenson County Historical Society of Freeport, Illinois, for finding a much needed letter from a member of the Oyler family. While it does not prove the event actually happened, it does prove the family legend. What a treasure!

Cindy Van Horn at The Lincoln Museum Research Library in Fort

Wayne, Indiana is invaluable during a research hunt. She always knows exactly where to locate an answer to a question, no matter how obscure it may seem.

Sincere thanks go to Tim Townsend and Susan Haake at the Lincoln Home National Historic Site for helping find the perfect photographs of the home's interior. I greatly appreciate the time they spent chatting about china, stoves, and wallpaper. I also thank them for putting me in touch with Sue Richter of the Vermillion County Museum, who helped date old photographs of the Lincoln Home, and Michelle Ganz at Lincoln Memorial University, who provided photos of Lincoln china.

My deepest gratitude goes to Kim M. Bauer, Director of the Lincoln Heritage Project in Decatur, Illinois, and former curator of the Lincoln collection for that state. He has become one of my "go-to" people when I can not find the answer to a Lincoln question. He either knows the answer or is able to shove me in the direction of the right answer. I am also deeply grateful to him for writing the foreword for this book. Kim's support and encouragement through this project and others are much appreciated.

When developing a manuscript, it is a pleasure to be able to call upon the expertise of friends, and I appreciate everything many of mine did to bring this book to completion. William Ciampa of Abe's Antiques in Gettysburg, Pennsylvania, allowed use of selected photographs from his vast private collection of White House and Washington, DC, images. Special photographs were also obtained from the late Mary Genevieve Townsend Murphy, who will always be an honorary member of the Todd clan.

In addition to new photographs, this edition needed fresh art work. Amy Castleberry provided the sketches used as section dividers and on the cover. I have enjoyed her art work and her friendship for years and was delighted she was available when asked to produce these sketches. My sincerest thanks go to her for her ability to work quickly and under pressure.

Greta Ratliff aided in both editions of *Lincoln's Table*. She offered advice, French translations, her nineteenth-century cookbook collection, and some taste-testing. I have relied upon her knowledge of the nineteenth-century

173

women's sphere many times over the years. She is truly an expert in all aspects—cooking, mourning, domestic life, and fashion.

Other friends who helped with the first edition and this one were Donna Daniels and Valerie Gugala. These two women are my friends and my cohorts. Together, we make up our own unique coterie dedicated to the study of Mary Lincoln. Among the three of us exists a vast Lincoln library. I am grateful they are willing to search theirs when a tidbit or documentation eludes me. They both helped tremendously, especially Valerie, who on more than one occasion was willing to keep searching well past 10:30. Many thanks go to both of these special women, and to the men in our lives who sit back and enjoy the ride when we are fortunate enough to be together.

What is a cookbook without a cook? Chef Eric Ramge helped decipher unusual cooking terms and ingredients, as well as providing much-needed baking directions that previously did not exist. Everyone who bakes or partakes of one of the historic recipes will be grateful that Chef Eric was able to modernize them. To him, we are all grateful.

Thanks to Karen Kennedy of Design in Bloom, Indianapolis, who designed an eye-popping dust jacket. Finally, a huge thank you goes to my editor and book designer Sheila Samson of WordCrafter, Inc., in Carmel, Indiana. Her creative eye takes plain words on a page and turns them into a work of art. Thank you for all of your help and patience, and thank you for your friendship.

Donna McCreary
May 2008

Bilbliography

Books

Anderson, Jean. *Recipes from American's Restored Villages.* New York: Doubleday and Co., 1975.

Angle, Paul M. *Life of Herndon's Lincoln.* New York: DaCapo Press, Inc. 1983.

Babette, "Aunt," *Aunt Babette's Cookbook.* Cincinnati: Block Publishers and Printing Company, 1889.

Baker, Jean H. *Mary Todd Lincoln: A Biography.* New York: W. W. Norton & Company, 1987.

Basler, Roy P., ed. *The Collected Works of Abraham Lincoln.* New Brunswick, NJ: Rutgers University Press, 1953.

Barnes, Bertha. *Antique Cook Book.* Harlan, Kentucky: Durham Printing and Offset, 1974.

Betty Crocker's Cookbook. New York: Prentice Hall, 1991.

Brooks, Noah. *Washington, DC, in Lincoln's Time,* edited with introduction and new preface by Herbert Mitgang. New York: Collier Books. 1962.

Carpenter, F. B. *The Inner Life of Abraham Lincoln: Six Months at the White House,* Introduction by Mark Neely Jr. Lincoln. Nebraska: University of Nebraska Press, 1995.

Carr, Richard Wallace, and Mary Pinak Carr. *The Willard Hotel: An Illustrated History.* Washington, DC: Dicmar Trading Co., 1986.

Cannon, Poppy, and Patricia Brooks. *The Presidents' Cookbook.* New York: Funk and Wagnalls, 1968.

Conway, W. Fred. *Young Abe Lincoln: His Teenage Yeas in Indiana.* New Albany, IN: FBH Publishers, 1992.

Donald, David Herbert. *Lincoln.* New York: Simon & Schuster, 1995.

Doty, William Kavanaugh. *The Confectionery of Monsieur Giron.* Lexington, Kentucky: The King Library Press, 1915. Reprinted with afterword by Burton Milward, 1978.

Editors of Favorite Recipes Press. *The Illustrated Encyclopedia of American Cooking.* Nashville, TN: Southwestern Company, 1992.

Ervin, Janet Halliday. *The White House Cookbook.* Chicago: Follett Publishing, 1964.

Eskew, Garnett Laidlaw, assisted by B. P. Adams. *Willard's of Washington: The Epic of a Capital Caravansary.* New York: Coward–McCann, Inc., 1954

Flexner, Marion. W. *Out of Kentucky Kitchens.* Lexington: University Press of Kentucky, 1989.

French, Marian. *Lincoln Heritage Trail Cookbook.* Williamsburg, VA: Bi-Cast Publishers, 1992. Reprinted 1994.

Fox, Minnie C. *The Blue Grass Cookbook.* New York, NY: Fox, Duffield & Co., 1904.

Gillette, Mrs. F. L. and Hugo Ziemann. *The White House Cookbook.* Chicago: RS Peale & Co., 1887.

Hale, Sarah Josepha. *Early American Cookery: The Good Housekeeper, 1841.* Mineola, New York: Dover Publications, Inc. Reprint edition, 1996.

Haller, Henry. *The White House Family Cookbook.* New York: Random House, 1987.

Harland, Marion. *Breakfast, Luncheon and Tea.* New York: Scribner, Armstrong & Co., 1875.

Hearn, Lafcadio. *La Cuisine Creole.* New Orleans: F. F. Hansell & Bros. Ltd., 1885.

Helm, Katherine. *Mary Wife of Lincoln.* New York: Harper & Brothers Publishers, 1928.

Holzer, Harold, ed. *Lincoln As I knew Him.* Chapel Hill, North Carolina: Algonquin Books of Chapel Hill, 1999.

Jones, Robert. *The Presidents' Own White House Cookbook.* Chicago: Culinary Arts Institute, 1973.

Leslie, Eliza. *Directions for Cookery, In It's Various Branches.* Philadelphia, PA: E. L. Carey & Hart, 1840.

McCully, Helen, ed. *American Heritage Cookbook.* New York: American Heritage Publishing, 1964.

Miers, Earl Schenck, and William E. Baringer, eds. *Lincoln Day by Day: A Chronology, 1809–1865, Volume I and Volume II.* Dayton, OH: Morningside, 1991.

Pratt, Harry E. *The Personal Finances of Abraham Lincoln.* Springfield, IL: The Abraham Lincoln Association, 1943

Randall, Ruth Painter. *Mary Lincoln, Biography of a Marriage.* Boston: Little, Brown and Company, 1953.

Randolph, Mary. *The Virginia Housewife, or Methodical Cook*. New York: Dover Publishers, Inc., (reprint) 1993.

Sanderson, J. M. *The Complete Cookbook*. Philadelphia: J.B. Lippincott, 1864.

Searcher, Victor. *Lincoln's Journey to Greatness*. Philadelphia: John Winston Company, 1960.

Smith, Myrtle Ellison. *Civil War Cookbook*. Harogate, TN: Lincoln Memorial University, 1962.

Spaulding, Lilly May, and John Spaulding, eds. *Civil War Recipes: Receipts from the Pp. of Godey's Lady's Book*. Lexington, KY: University Press of Kentucky, 1999.

Stoner, Carol Hupping, ed. *Stocking Up: How to Preserve the Foods You Grow Naturally*. Emmaus, PA: Rodal Press, 1977.

Temple, Wayne C. *The Taste Is in My Mouth A Little. . . Lincoln's Victuals and Potables*. Mahomet, IL: Mayhaven Publishing, 2004.

Townsend, William H. *Lincoln and the Bluegrass: Slavery and Civil War in Kentucky*. Lexington: University Press of Kentucky, 1955.

Turner, Justin G, and Linda Levitt Turner: *Mary Todd Lincoln: Her Life and Letters*. New York: Alfred A. Knopf, 1972.

Warren, Louis A. *Lincoln's Youth, Indiana Years, 1816–1830*. Indianapolis: Indiana Historical Society, reprint 1991.

Wilson, Douglas L. and Rodney O. Davis, ed. *Herndon's Informants: Letters, Interviews and Statements about Abraham Lincoln*. Champaign, IL: University of Illinois Press, 1998.

MANUSCRIPTS, NEWSPAPERS, AND OTHER SOURCES

Arnold, Isaac N. Address before Illinois State Bar Association, Springfield, IL, January 7, 1881. *History of Sangamon County, Illinois*. Chicago. Inter-State Publishing Co. 1881. Reprint Evansville, IN: Unigraphic, INC. 1977.

Bernard, Kenneth A. "Lincoln and the Music of the Civil War, VIII, Will the Leader of the Band Please See Mrs. Lincoln?" *Lincoln Herald*, Spring 1962.

Chicago Tribune (Special to the *New York Herald*) February 5, 1862.

Chicago Tribune (Special to the *New York Tribune*) February 10, 1862.

Frank Leslie's Illustrated Newspaper, February 22, 1862, p. 209.

Food Down Under: www.FoodDownUnder.com.

Grimsley, Elizabeth Todd, "Six Months in the White House," *Journal of the Illinois State Historical Society*, Vol. XIX, October 1926–January 1927, Nos. 3–4, Springfield, IL.

Helm Family Papers. Kentucky Historical Society, Frankfort, KY.

Hickey, James. "Lincolniana: The Lincoln Account at the Corneau and Diller Drug Store 1849–1861," *Journal of the Illinois State Historical Society*. Vol. 77, Spring 1984, pp. 60–66. Springfield, IL.

Illinois Journal, Vol. VII, No. 206, January 31, 1855, Page 3. Column 1.

Jacob Bunn Ledger, 1849, Manuscript Collection BV, Abraham Lincoln Presidential Library, Springfield, IL.

King, Caroline B. "Famous Dishes from the Old Kentucky Home," *The Ladies' Home Journal*, c. 1923, pp. 143–144.

Lincoln, Robert Todd Collection, Folder 7 of 11, Chicago History Museum.

"Mary Lincoln Vertical File" Drawer 2, The Lincoln Museum, Fort Wayne, IN.

New Orleans Daily Delta, April 9, 1862, and *The National Telegraph* of Clarksburg, WVa, February 14, 1862.

Stuart/Hay Family Papers 1817–1892. Letter from John Todd Stuart to his daughter Elizabeth Stuart, Sunday, June 2, 1856. Manuscript Department, ALPL, Springfield, IL.

Townsend, William H. Collection. Helm Family Papers. King Library, University of Kentucky, Lexington, KY.

Watson, J.W. "With Four Great Men," *North American Revue*, Vol. 147, No. 5, November 1888.

Index

Index of Recipes